Josep M. Benet i Jornet

TWO PLAYS

Josep M. Benet i Jornet

Photo: courtesy of the playwright

Josep M. Benet i Jornet

Two Plays

Fleeting

Stages

Translated
by
Marion Peter Holt

Martin E. Segal Theatre Center Publications
New York
© 2008

Library of Congress Cataloging-in-Publication Data

Benet i Jornet, Josep Maria, 1940-
[Fugaç. English]
Two plays : Fleeting ; Stages / Josep M. Benet i Jornet ; translated from Catalan by Marion Peter Holt.
    p. cm.
ISBN 978-0-9790570-5-2
I. Holt, Marion Peter. II. Benet i Jornet, Josep Maria, 1940- E.R. English. III. Title. IV. Title: E.R.
PC3942.12.E47F8413 2008
849'.9254--dc22

2008047003

The translation of this work has been supported with a grant from the Institut Ramon Llull.

Fugaç (Fleeting) © 1995 by Josep M. Benet i Jornet, translation © 2007 by Marion Peter Holt. E.R. (Stages) © 1994 by Josep M. Benet i Jornet, translation © 2001 by Marion Peter Holt.

Copy-editing, typography, and design by Christopher Silsby
Cover design by Christopher Silsby and Marion Peter Holt

© 2008 Martin E. Segal Theatre Center
Daniel Gerould, Executive Director
Frank Hentschker, Director of Programs
Jan Stenzel, Director of Administration

TRANSLATOR'S DEDICATION

In memory of Puck, a much loved Catalan feline friend.

TABLE OF CONTENTS

Pep Cruz and Meritxell Sabater in *Fugaç* (*Fleeting*),
Teatre Romea (1994), directed by Rosa Maria Sardà.
Photo: courtesy of the playwright

PREFACE

Josep M. Benet i Jornet was born in Barcelona's working-class Raval neighborhood two years after the end of the Spanish Civil War. The triumphant Nationalist forces had occupied the starving city and suppressed all expression of Catalan culture, even forbidding the public use of the Catalan language. Twenty-five years later, in 1964, the young playwright would be the first recipient of the Josep M. de Sagarra Prize for Drama in Catalan, and he would see his play *Una vella, coneguda olor* (*An Old, Familiar Smell*) staged at the historic Teatre Romea by a cast of professional actors and theatre students. Still, opportunities for future stagings were decidedly limited during the restrictive Franco dictatorship. In 1972, he experienced harsh and painful rejection of his most ambitious play up to that point, the inventive *Berenàveu a les fosques* (*You Were Lunching in the Dark*), in which he had combined techniques considered Brechtian (scenic projections and scene titles) and fluid temporal development with an essentially realistic mode. It was a bitter disappointment, but Benet continued to write works in which he experimented with form and theme. *La desaparició de Wendy* (*The Disappearance of Wendy*), 1973, is a postmodernist integration of characters from children's literature into a totally original play about the power of theatrical representation; *Descripció de un paisatge* (*Description of a Landscape*), 1977-78, resets the myth of Hecuba in a contemporary Muslim society.

Only after the staging by Madrid's Centro Dramático Nacional in 1980 of his *Motín de brujas*, a Spanish version of *Revolta de bruixes* (*Witches Revolt*), written between 1971 and 1975, did he begin to receive widespread recognition throughout Spain. A striking aspect of this play was the use of simultaneous, overlapping speeches and multiple stories which required actors responsive to an unfamiliar style and direction that accommodated it. The playwright later wrote in an introduction to *Witches Revolt* that he had now broken with established conventions of the past to pursue his own concepts of realistic drama. It was a prime example of his departure from the familiar in unexpected and original ways to challenge his audiences. Benet has demonstrated increasing daring in the use of structural innovations in thematically provocative plays, including *Desig* (*Desire*), 1991, *Fugaç* (*Fleeting*), 1994, *E.R.* (*Stages*), 1994, and *Testament* (*Legacy*), 1996; and in 2003, Barcelona's

Teatre Lliure, staged one of his most memorable works, *L'habitació del nen* (*The Child's Room*), in which two views of "reality" are presented in contrasting scenes.

In 2005, the controversial *Salamandra* was staged at the Teatre Nacional de Catalunya, under the direction of Toni Casares. The theme of the play was potential extinction—of a family line, of the Catalan language, of Western civilization. Intertextually woven into the play was the legend of the salamander that is regenerated after destruction by fire, and a wounded, nearly extinct breed of salamander provides a striking visual symbol in several scenes of the play. The playwright's dramatic adaptation of Mercè Rodoreda's classic novel *La plaça del diamant* was staged by the Teatre Nacional de Catalunya in 2007, and his "chamber" play *Soterrani* (*Underground*) had its premiere in 2008 at the Sala Beckett. Today Benet i Jornet is considered one of the most original voices in contemporary European theatre, and his plays are performed in many languages throughout the world. In Catalonia, he has been a major contributor to Barcelona's increasingly vibrant and diverse theatre scene.

Fleeting and *Stages*

Fugaç (*Fleeting*) can well be viewed as a tragedy-within-a-play, since the second act is the depiction of an incestuous relationship between a father and a daughter, framed by what appears to be a more conventional drama about personal dissatisfactions and anxieties in contemporary society. A group of friends and acquaintances, including a doctor and his wife, have gathered for an evening dinner at a suburban home and for diversion they sit around a séance table that is a family heirloom belonging to the hostess. Even when the table taps out the letters that spell "death," the audience may only assume that it is an ordinary suspense element introduced by the playwright. The doctor leaves early—supposedly to attend a patient but actually to join his daughter at their home. In the second act, their impossible relationship does indeed end in death for both. Through a masterful melding of form and content, spectators find themselves jolted from the seemingly familiar and predictable to an unsuspected and inadmissible reality. In the third act of *Fleeting,* which is taking place in the same time frame as the "tragedy," the characters at the country home have found solutions to their problems as they sit watching the night sky, and the greatest concern of the doctor's wife is the mundane inconvenience of re-doing her kitchen next day. But the audience already knows that her comfortable and safe existence has been permanently shattered, and thus her casual, final monologue becomes painfully ironic. Benet has experimented throughout his career with innovative uses of traditional dramatic formulas to create a totally personal restructuring, and the combination of tragedy and domestic drama with simultaneous actions make *Fleeting* a unique and disturbing theatrical experience.

In 1979, Benet wrote a definitive introduction for the publication of what is perhaps the most complex and daring Catalan play of the 1970s, Rodolf Sirera's *Plany en la mort d'Enric Ribera* (*Lament on the Death of Enric Ribera*). Benet's fascination with this work about the life and death of the fictional actor Enric Ribera, inspired in part by the career and political and sexual ambiguity of the Nobel Prize recipient Jacinto Benavente, was apparent in the insights he brought to his analysis. Some fourteen years later, he paid further tribute to Sirera's play by writing a new work, *E. R.* (*Stages*), in which the deceased sister of Enric Ribera, Empar, becomes the off-stage inspiration for a young acting student who, in preparation for a play about the fabled actress, is attempting to discover insights into her life by interviewing three of her former students. They now have their own careers in theatre, television, and film-dubbing respectively, and their memories of past events vary considerably and reflect their own degree of self-dramatization. While Sirera was experimenting with words arranged in musical patterns to replicate symphonic movements, Benet provides less obvious but subtle musical analogies in three thematic variations of the same story as recalled in differing narrative monologues. A theatrically riveting coda completes the play when the disillusioned younger actress burns a toy theatre that had once belonged to the dead Empar and also features the identifying letters *E.R.* (the initials of Empar Ribera). *E. R.* became one of Benet's most successful and admired plays following its premiere at Barcelona's Teatre Lliure in 1994. Stagings in Madrid (1998) and in several Latin American cities followed when the play was translated into Spanish; in 1996, Catalan film director Ventura Pons brought the play to the screen as *Actrius* (*Actresses*), with a cast that included leading performers Nuria Espert and Rosa Maria Sardà, as well as the Teatre Lliure stalwart Anna Lizaran. Although this play deals compellingly with theatre and its force upon the people who create theatre, it not strictly a Pirandellian work; rather it brings to mind Kurosawa's film *Rashomon*, in which characters recall their own differing versions of the past and demonstrate the illusiveness of memory.

About the Translations

The translation of *Fugaç* is based on the edition published by Editorial Lumen following the first production of the play at Barcelona's Teatre Romea in 1994. That of *E.R.* is based on Edicions 62's third edition of the text (1997), first published in 1994 at the time of the premiere at the Teatre Lliure. The title of the English version of *E.R.*, *Stages*, was chosen to avoid the associations that English-speaking audiences and readers might have with the letters "E.R." I am mindful, however, that these initials are subtly encoded in the play's text, and directors have the option of using the original title whenever the play is staged.

M.P.H.

FLEETING

A Play by

Josep M. Benet i Jornet

Translated by

Marion Peter Holt

CHARACTERS

Wife

Doctor

Son

Lady of the House

Young Woman

Friend

Girl

ACT ONE

Informal Interior

It is still daylight, but soon it will grow dark. At a point in the action the lights should be turned on. The DOCTOR, *age 50, and the* WIFE, *age 46.*

WIFE: What were you dreaming about last night?

DOCTOR: I don't remember.

WIFE: You were talking in your sleep.

DOCTOR: What was I saying?

WIFE: I couldn't understand you. You seemed happy.

DOCTOR: I fell fast asleep.

WIFE: It's a nice afternoon. The heat's dry.

DOCTOR: Yes.

WIFE: Look. (SHE *points.*) Isn't it lovely? We find it easy to speak of unpleasant things and it embarrasses us to talk about beauty. Happiness should be acknowledged too.

DOCTOR: I acknowledge that I love you.

WIFE: This moment . . . Nothing special . . . I'm here, I see all that, you beside me, fine. She's at home, that's fine too; and the others ready to help me spend a pleasant evening. What more could I ask? (HE *pulls her toward him.*) What's with you? Let go. If someone came in, they'd have a good laugh. A middle-aged married couple making out in a corner.

DOCTOR: You're warm. Your body's warm.

WIFE: The heat bothers you.

DOCTOR: No. Your body's just right to be against mine. Are you really glad you came?

WIFE: Are you sorry you persuaded me to?

DOCTOR: I shouldn't have insisted. I won't be able to stay myself.

WIFE: I can only say that it's fine with me . . . What did you think? That I feel one thing and say another? Don't worry.

DOCTOR: I won't stay long. I can't, can I?

WIFE: Whether you can or won't, it's all the same. I'll stay because I'd like to. You need to go, so it's better for you to go.

DOCTOR: What are you thinking when you say that?

WIFE: I'm thinking that you should relax. Now repeat that you love me.

DOCTOR: I love you.

WIFE: You see? Everything's fine. Don't you really remember what you dreamed?

DOCTOR: Nothing at all.

WIFE: You were saying . . . it seemed like names.

DOCTOR: Yours?

WIFE: Perhaps mine, too. Everything's set. We'll have dinner and it will be enjoyable. You can leave quietly. (SHE *listens*.) I think someone's just arrived.

The WIFE *exits. The* DOCTOR *picks up a small leather bag.* HE *opens it, takes out some pharmaceutical products and doctors' instruments, some of them metallic and aggressive looking, and slowly puts them back in. Mechanically* HE *arranges, beside the bag, a bottle of pills, another with an injectable substance, and a syringe. HE looks at the little collection as if looking into space. A* YOUNG MAN *of 32 enters.*

SON: The doctor and his medicines that solve everything.

DOCTOR: (*Returning to reality, smiles.*) I don't know what I was thinking. (HE *puts away the objects he had lined up.*) Your artist friend has arrived, right?

SON: Yes, he's here now. If he's not very talkative or says something silly, I hope you'll be patient with him.

DOCTOR: Is that an order?

SON: I'll try to do likewise, if I can. It's a favor we'll do for him.

DOCTOR: And why must we do him a favor?

SON: Weaknesses of his.

DOCTOR: What's wrong?

SON: Why should there be anything wrong with me?

DOCTOR: With your friend, I mean.

SON: I don't know if I should try to explain it. He doesn't want anyone to know. Well, it's all the same, but don't mention I've told you. He has submitted a model of a large sculpture that's to go in some public square or other. He is one of only two candidates. Today they decide who gets the commission.

DOCTOR: So he just has a case of nerves.

SON: It's a moment of crisis in his life and a project that can be important for his career.

DOCTOR: I wonder if his career is all about becoming famous.

SON: I hope that's not everything. He's beginning to feel old, there are younger artists who're coming on strong and are more modish. He's not talked about as much as he used to be, people aren't calling him as they used to. I don't think his problem is becoming famous but rather holding on to what he's achieved.

DOCTOR: I don't know whether you're blaming him or justifying him.

SON: I'm justifying myself. I picked a good moment for all of us to get together. I'm a saint.

DOCTOR: Of course, but now you've lost me.

SON: Basically, I invited you and your wife for his sake, to get his mind off things. He had told me that he'd like to take advantage of the occasion to try the thing with the table. I don't know if I've done the right thing.

DOCTOR: Well, I suppose I'll have to meet him.

THEY *exit. The* LADY *of the house and the doctor's* WIFE *enter.*

LADY: There's a helper who comes every day. You think I need anyone else? I don't. Do you see how lucky I am to live alone? You don't have to give explanations to anyone. You come and go as you please. You tell the cleaning lady what you want and the more selfish you are the better. A selfish, controlling, old woman who gives orders to her hired help. I treat her well, of course, but I treat myself even better. I just don't have to give reasons. First I lost my husband. I thought I would die before him. And then my son, when he decided to get his own place. Now it's the whole house just for me. Plenty of space. If you find yourself in the same situation someday, you'll know what I mean, it's like being reborn. Oh, I'm sorry, I didn't realize how much I was talking.

WIFE: Don't worry, it's fine. You're absolutely right.

LADY: I'm so glad you've come. I'm so happy to see you both. I hope you don't regret it.

WIFE: Don't talk nonsense. But, my husband . . . As you know, he wanted to stay all evening, but something came up.

A YOUNG WOMAN *of 28 enters with a tray of poorly arranged glasses in precarious equilibrium.*

YOUNG WOMAN: Eeeh, they're going to fall! Get out of my way or they'll fall and break. I must be an utter idiot to try to bring them all at once. Where can I put them? What am I doing?

LADY: They're not going to fall, they won't.

YOUNG WOMAN: I knew this would happen the moment I picked up the tray. Just my luck! Let me by!

LADY: Just give me the tray!

YOUNG WOMAN: I'm a fool, I break everything I touch! They're slipping off!

LADY: Over here, easy. Let me give you a hand.

WIFE: Let her help.

YOUNG WOMAN: My God, I must look ridiculous.

LADY: Just be calm. Down, slowly, fine. You see? You haven't broken a thing.

YOUNG WOMAN: Nothing.

WIFE: What happened to you?

YOUNG WOMAN: Hysteria. Some way to present myself to people. Who knows what came over me. Don't worry, I won't be like this all evening. That would be too much! I'll try to behave like a good girl. There's no need to make such a fuss, right?

LADY: Are you all right now?

YOUNG WOMAN: Of course. Don't pay me any attention. What else should I bring in?

LADY: We have lots of time. And I'm the one who'll be serving. Come along, let's both go.

The LADY *and The* YOUNG WOMAN *exit. The* DOCTOR *enters.*

DOCTOR: How are things going?

WIFE: There's a certain excitement in the air.

The SON *and his* FRIEND, *age 38, enter from the same direction as the* DOCTOR.

SON. A drink? We'll have something before dinner.

DOCTOR: I'm not staying for dinner. I can't. I'm sorry.

SON: Come now, you must.

DOCTOR: What can I say?

SON: My mother will be sorry to hear that.

WIFE: We're sorry, too. But I'm staying.

SON: I wouldn't want to be a doctor and be on call at all hours. Here are the glasses but no drinks.

FRIEND: Thanks to that old excuse about seeing a sick patient, you doctors always have a handy alibi.

WIFE: He's never needed an alibi with me.

A moment and then SHE *exits.*

DOCTOR: Actually I don't have to visit patients. I want to get home in time to see my daughter before she goes to bed. She's going away tomorrow.

SON: On a trip?

DOCTOR: Precisely. If I don't see her tonight, I won't see her at all.

FRIEND: I've never been married and I've never wanted to have children. I have the impression they tie you down.

DOCTOR: Quite a lot!

FRIEND: I know I'm not one to set an example.

The LADY, the WIFE, and the YOUNG WOMAN enter with bottles. Without stopping, the WIFE continues off on the opposite side with the FRIEND.

LADY: The drinks.

The SON tried to help the YOUNG WOMAN.

YOUNG WOMAN: Don't bother. You might tire yourself.

SON: What's wrong with you?

YOUNG WOMAN: Don't you know?

SON: Huh?

YOUNG WOMAN: That's what's wrong with me, that you don't know what's wrong.

The DOCTOR, the LADY, and the YOUNG WOMAN leave. The SON crosses to his FRIEND and the WIFE, who have returned.

WIFE: (*To the SON, referring to the FRIEND.*) I've shown him the table.

FRIEND: It looks like an innocent piece of furniture.

WIFE: Have you really never made tables move around?

FRIEND: Never.

WIFE: It's very entertaining, you'll see.

SON: At least someone will be entertained.

WIFE: So will you, I suppose.

SON: That's why I organized this dinner, but I don't know, some things have happened, at the last minute. It was rather difficult for us to leave and drive out to my mother's house.

FRIEND: I appreciate your frankness.

SON: No, no. It had nothing to do with either of you. Domestic problems. The truth is, children tie you down.

WIFE: Why did you mention your children?

FRIEND: I've always said I didn't want to have any.

WIFE: No? You're an artist, and artists should try everything.

SON: And you also have to try your hand at the art of making the table dance.

FRIEND: Artists are misunderstood and unappreciated, didn't you know that?

SON: Yes, go on and complain. They'll give you the commission for the sculpture and then you'll have to admit that you're appreciated.

WIFE: What sculpture is that?

FRIEND: Just a sculpture. Nothing.

SON: I suppose they know what you're keeping to yourself.

FRIEND: Maybe they do. Do you mind if we change the subject. (*To the* WIFE.) It has to do with my work, but when I came I left it all at the door with my coat.

The LADY, *the* YOUNG WOMAN, *and the* DOCTOR *return.*

DOCTOR: She says that some chairs and a serving cart have to be moved.

LADY: Stay right where you are, I'll go, don't move.

FRIEND: Do we bring them here?

SON: To the dining room, I suppose.

LADY: Just relax if you don't want to upset me.

DOCTOR: Let's go help, what do you say?

SON: It'll only take a moment.

The DOCTOR, *the* SON, *and the* FRIEND *exit.*

LADY: Making the guests work, that's what you'll say.

YOUNG WOMAN: A little work won't hurt them.

LADY: You're upset. What has that son of mine done to you?

YOUNG WOMAN: Nothing.

LADY: Forgive me if I hit a sore spot.

WIFE: I'll go oversee things.

YOUNG WOMAN: Stay, please. I have no secrets you can't hear. (*To the* LADY.) Did you overhear us when we were quarreling?

LADY: You're tense. Maybe I'm to blame.

YOUNG WOMAN: How can you think that? My problem is I overreact to things. I can't hide my feelings. I give importance to little things that are laughable. I make them seem important. I can't help it. If I tell you what's wrong, don't laugh at me afterwards. Anyone who doesn't have problems goes looking for them.

LADY: There's nothing that isn't important.

YOUNG WOMAN: Here it is in a nutshell. Six years ago your son and I made our commitment to each other. Six years ago today.

LADY: Really? How time flies.

YOUNG WOMAN: He wasn't the first man in my life, he was the third, and there's been no one else.

LADY: He loves you, too.

YOUNG WOMAN: He always remembered the anniversary every year. Every year there was some kind of gift. The gifts don't matter to me. Remembering does. And today, for the first time, there hasn't been a gift.

LADY: Now I understand.

YOUNG WOMAN: And I've been getting hysterical. For no reason, I know. Anyone can be forgetful. And even if it's only forgetfulness, it's all the same. I'm behaving like a spoiled child.

LADY: I'll kill that son of mine.

YOUNG WOMAN: Don't you dare say a thing to him!

LADY: How stupid of him, what a lack of feeling!

WIFE: From the outside, it looks simpler to me. You can't judge a man by one act of forgetfulness, it doesn't seem fair to me.

YOUNG WOMAN: No, it's not such a big thing.

WIFE: No.

LADY: Yes, it is.

YOUNG WOMAN: No, she's right. It's just that I don't know myself. Do you know what's wrong with me?

LADY: You love my son.

YOUNG WOMAN: (*After a pause.*) Well, yes I do. Maybe too much. I love him a lot. After six years I still love him so much . . . Is it a mistake to love him that way?

LADY: It may be.

YOUNG WOMAN: No, don't say that. I don't regret it. And I'm not tired of loving him. But he . . . (*To the* LADY.) It's just that there are other things, not only the thing today. Don't be shocked if I tell you this, but . . . but in bed it's not the way it used to be. No, he doesn't want me the way he did before.

WIFE: And what did you expect? The same passion for a lifetime?

YOUNG WOMAN: No, but . . . I know and I keep telling myself that. I live watching him like someone who watches a vase, trying to keep it from getting broken, even though it will end up broken anyhow someday.

WIFE: Don't worry your head so much.

LADY: You both need some rest. A few weeks of relaxation together; that would relieve some of the tensions that have been building up. They always build up, it's inevitable. (*The* SON *and the* FRIEND *enter.*) Why don't you come here and bring the children? A few days of vacation. Where can you get better treatment? I won't be in the way, and I'll be the loving grandmother. (*To her* SON.) I'm not doing it for myself, I'm fine and happy here with my own activities. But it's a pity to have such a big house with only me to enjoy it.

SON: (*Impatient.*) Don't press it.

LADY: It would be very healthy for the children.

YOUNG WOMAN: (*Sarcastic.*) Keep off the topic of children and health if you don't mind.

LADY: But why?

YOUNG WOMAN: When it suits him, he can get overly concerned about the children, you have to admit.

SON: Don't start on that. I do worry about the children. So what? Especially when there's good reason.

LADY: And what's there to worry about now?

SON: Nothing. But the older one has a fever today.

LADY: Why didn't you tell me? Is it very high?

YOUNG WOMAN: Children get high fevers. The babysitter knows what to do and by now with the medication the fever's probably gone down.

SON: I knew from the start it was nothing, but the fever was awfully high. He'd already had it for a day when we took him to the pediatrician, and we hadn't been able to get it down even a degree. The doctor didn't say it wasn't serious.

YOUNG WOMAN: And he didn't say it was either.

SON: Let's not talk about it anymore, OK? Just leave me alone.

DOCTOR: If you need any professional help, just say so. I don't want you to be unnecessarily concerned.

YOUNG WOMAN: It's only a sore throat, as usual.

WIFE: Our daughter also used to have high fevers. Being a doctor's daughter didn't prevent it.

FRIEND: (*To the* SON.) And you wouldn't have wanted to come because of that?

SON: Can we just forget about it?

DOCTOR: It's getting dark.

WIFE: Is it evening already?

DOCTOR: Not quite. I'm going outside for a few minutes to get some air.

WIFE: It doesn't seem too warm to me.

YOUNG WOMAN: I think I'll go out, too.

The DOCTOR *and the* YOUNG WOMAN *exit.* SHE *has a glass in her hand.*

SON: (*Holding up the bottle.*) Anyone want more? (*The* WIFE *accepts a drink.*)

FRIEND: (*To the* LADY, *aside.*) It's possible they'll call here asking for me. I took the liberty of giving your phone number.

LADY: But of course.

WIFE: Aren't you having something? (*The* WIFE *and the* LADY *move aside.*)

SON: (*To the* FRIEND.) When do you think it'll be decided?

FRIEND: They've probably already made their decision.

SON: Forgive me for mentioning it in front of everyone.

FRIEND: Forgive me for being so abrupt with you. I don't want to worry about it.

SON: But you are worried.

FRIEND: (*Laughs.*) You think so?

HE *starts to leave just as the* YOUNG WOMAN *enters.*

SON: I've seen the two models, and yours is the best. Whatever happens, congratulations.

YOUNG WOMAN: Who's getting congratulated?

FRIEND: Me. But it's premature. (*Exits.*)

YOUNG WOMAN: Better premature than never. (*A brusque gesture. The glass breaks in her hand, or* SHE *drops it.*) I knew it.

LADY: It's nothing.

WIFE: It's good luck.

YOUNG WOMAN: What a mess. What have I spilled it on?

LADY: It doesn't matter. A broken glass is the least that can happen.

SON: I'd better pick up the pieces.

The DOCTOR *enters again. The* SON *picks up the shards and exits.*

YOUNG WOMAN: I knew it, a glass.

LADY: I'll go get a cloth to wipe up. (*Exits.*)

YOUNG WOMAN: No, I'm the one who should do that.

SHE *exits behind the* LADY. *The* DOCTOR *and his* WIFE *are left alone.* THEY *exchange looks.*

DOCTOR: A certain electricity in air, wouldn't you say? At any moment now they're going to start biting one another.

WIFE: Don't let them hear you.

DOCTOR: I'm sorry for you. You'll have to put up with them and you were expecting to enjoy yourself.

WIFE: I still haven't given up on enjoying myself.

DOCTOR: How do you plan to do that?

The SON *and the* FRIEND *enter.*

WIFE: I'll get to the point. Why don't we start setting up the table?

SON: Maybe we should.

DOCTOR: A good idea. Afterwards I'll have to go and I wouldn't want to miss the seance.

FRIEND: Try not to give away the trick so that I can try to figure it out for myself.

SON: There is no trick. Give me a hand.

The SON, *the* FRIEND, *and the* DOCTOR *move aside chairs and other pieces of furniture. The* YOUNG WOMAN *and the* LADY *return with the necessary items to clean up the glass and effects of the spill.*

LADY: Are you setting up the table already?

DOCTOR: Without your permission. Do you want us to wait?

LADY: No, no. Just move anything that's in the way.

YOUNG WOMAN: Give that to me, I'll take it. You stay here in case they need you.

SHE *exits, carrying off the refuse, the cleaning cloth, and whatever. The* SON, *the* FRIEND, *and the* DOCTOR *have cleared a space and exit, too.*

LADY: (*Goes to the* WIFE's *side.*) Who would need me? Nobody. Not for moving furniture or anything else.

WIFE: You shouldn't say that.

LADY: I said it as a joke, but it's true. Oh, God . . .

WIFE: What's wrong?

LADY: Nothing. There's never anything wrong with me, and to avoid getting bored, I think about things.

WIFE: Don't tell me you have problems, too.

LADY: What do you mean by "too"?

WIFE: I thought that at least you had been spared.

LADY: Who else has problems?

WIFE: Everyone. Tell me about yours.

LADY: I don't want to bore you. No, I don't have any problems. This house of mine is so very cozy. That's what they say. So cozy that sometimes the walls close in on me.

WIFE: I thought you loved living here. You said so just a while ago.

LADY: When I finish dusting, I sit in a chair and look at the ceiling.

WIFE: I don't believe it. If you don't stop, I'll think I don't know you any longer.

LADY: I miss having people around me. I talk to myself. No, I won't stop. I'm lucky. When I stop, there we are. Sounds echo in my head and I begin to hear voices and I know they're not real but I start to cry and one day I'll go mad. I'm already going mad.

WIFE: When you don't feel well, call your friends.

LADY: Hush, I couldn't. But I was hoping that my son would come here with the children to spend two or three weeks. Next year I'll be able to have them all to myself; at least one, he'll be old enough then. He'd have to want to come and not miss his parents. Don't ever wish to be alone, it's not good. It's the worst thing in life, to be obligated to other people. Why are you looking at me?

WIFE: I'm listening to you.

The SON, *the* FRIEND, *and the* DOCTOR *enter with a low table made of fine wood.*

LADY: Here I am complaining this very evening when I'm absolutely delighted with your company.

SON: The table is ready. I heard you, mama, and, yes, you at least can be absolutely delighted. The older boy has a fever, and I'm here as the dutiful son.

FRIEND: How should we sit? Do we have to place ourselves in any special order?

DOCTOR: Anywhere you like. Each one where they please. Right?

LADY: Take your pick, there are no ceremonies, no places of preference.

FRIEND: (*To the DOCTOR.*) Do you tell your patients that you make tables move?

DOCTOR: I've helped make one move three or four times in my life.

FRIEND: If they saw you, you would be a disgrace to science forever.

DOCTOR: What do you mean? Maybe I would. Look, I'm not going to feel guilty.

The YOUNG WOMAN *enters.*

YOUNG WOMAN: What have you done? Oh, the table.

WIFE: We're going to begin.

YOUNG WOMAN: Make a place for me.

LADY: All of you sit down. Now, be very calm, all right?

FRIEND: Should we keep silent?

YOUNG WOMAN: We need a bit of concentration.

LADY: At least as a start.

FRIEND: Do you always take charge?

LADY: Not necessarily.

YOUNG WOMAN: Almost always.

SON: By tradition.

WIFE: She does it better than anyone.

DOCTOR: She's an expert.

LADY: Now, don't make me nervous. All right. Listen as I speak and relax. Get rid of your nerves. Relax, let yourself go. Your hands wide on the table . . .

FRIEND: Like this?

LADY: Spread wide and gently on the table. The thumb of one hand touching the thumb of the other hand and your little fingers touching the little fingers of the persons to the right and left of you. Let me see. That's very good. Relax, concentrate . . . Everyone concentrate . . .

FRIEND: What do we do?

SON: We don't do anything.

LADY: Be quiet . . . and no laughing. The spirits want respect and peace. Excuse me, my son doesn't believe in spirits. He only believes in the table. If you don't believe in spirits, at least accept it as an innocent game: it harms no one. How many people must have sat around this table over the years . . . I always saw it at our home. I don't know where it came from. My father would make it dance. Sometimes, when our rowdiness got out of hand, he'd grab the four children and make us sit this way, just as we are now. Don't laugh, please, don't let your attention stray from the table. We would sit and you should have seen how seriously we took it. The table would start moving. I remember that emotion. We would ask questions. Suddenly our problems would come out, our peeves, and our desires. We were children with worries, there are always things to worry about, and the table answered us. One tap means yes, two taps mean no. The table would begin to move, not like a toy that you wind up, but like some live thing you've awakened. My father conducted the game. Our worries and concerns. Those that we all knew about and those that only one of us knew. Children's concerns. My father wouldn't laugh. Never. And with the table order was restored. The table did it. Or my father and the table. Or the spirits. (*Change of tone.*) Look!

WIFE: What?

LADY: It's moving.

SON: There we are. It's started.

FRIEND: Who's moving it?

SON: Thoughts.

DOCTOR: It moves by itself.

YOUNG WOMAN: An energy.

WIFE: We don't know which.

FRIEND: You mean, without any reason?

DOCTOR: For the moment, yes.

LADY: Spirits, maybe.

SON: Mother.

LADY: Let the table tap once. (*An energetic tap.*) Let the table tap twice. (*Two energetic taps.*) We can begin, the table is ready.

FRIEND: You all do it very well, I'm fascinated.

LADY: Who's going to ask first?

SON: (*To the* FRIEND.) You ask, it's really for you.

FRIEND: What kind of question?

LADY: Any kind you wish.

YOUNG WOMAN: First you ask something simple, to see how it goes.

FRIEND: How many brothers and sisters do I have, how old am I . . . ?

DOCTOR: . . . How many loves you've had in your life, what are we, where do we come from, where are we going.

LADY: Shhhhh.

SON: Begin.

YOUNG WOMAN: Don't be afraid.

FRIEND: You're playing a joke on me.

SON: All right, I enjoy it, I'll ask.

FRIEND: No, wait. I'll ask. Does the table know how to count?

LADY: Yes.

FRIEND: Table, how many people are seated around you?

Six taps.

LADY: Six taps, six people.

FRIEND: A very clever table. Let's do another. Did I get up in a good mood today?

Two taps.

LADY: No.

FRIEND: That was easy to guess.

LADY: The table guessed it.

SON: What you know the table knows.

FRIEND: It was easy. and you guessed right. Choosing the most probable. You're intelligent people.

YOUNG WOMAN: It's no trick.

FRIEND: I'll catch you.

SON: Is it my turn now?

FRIEND: No, not yet. A more difficult question. Let's see . . .

LADY: What?

DOCTOR: The more brilliant the question, the more brilliant the answer.

FRIEND: Brilliant?

DOCTOR: Don't you like brilliant answers?

FRIEND: I don't like lies. What about you?

DOCTOR: (*Smiles.*) It depends.

LADY: Actually, no one likes lies.

YOUNG WOMAN: Back to the table, please.

FRIEND: Haven't you looked around you? Here we are smiling, polite, talking and having drinks . . . Ask the table: which of us is suffering most at this moment?

The LADY, *the* SON, *and the* YOUNG WOMAN *take their hands off the table. Immediately, the* FRIEND *will do the same. During the succeeding dialogue, only the*

DOCTOR *and the* WIFE *will keep their hands more or less in their original position.*

YOUNG WOMAN: No, please. I didn't think you were that kind of person.

SON: There's no reason to upset anyone.

FRIEND: Don't you dare?

LADY: There's no reason. It doesn't matter who suffers or doesn't suffer.

FRIEND: If we don't spice things up a bit, there's no excitement. And without a bit of excitement, what's the point of playing?

LADY: I, for one, have respect for the table.

FRIEND: Maybe you'll convince me and I'll respect it, too. My question wasn't intended maliciously. Besides, who will the table indicate? Maybe me, if you all agree to it. The hunter hunted. So what? It's all the same to me, the point is to amuse ourselves.

YOUNG WOMAN: You really would love to know that you're suffering more than anyone and for us to know it. Well, have it your way.

SON: No.

WIFE: Wait. It really doesn't seem like such a bad question.

DOCTOR: I agree with my wife.

WIFE: Everyone is free to ask what they wish.

SON: You're looking for trouble, aren't you?

LADY: We begin laughing and end up crying.

FRIEND: I'm not looking for anything.

LADY: We're wasting too much time. Let him ask.

WIFE: Ask your question.

LADY: One moment. Your hands, make sure they're touching. Fingers against fingers. All right, now ask.

Pause.

FRIEND: Which of us is suffering most at this moment?

Short pause. Suddenly the table moves, hesitates, and ends up making a quick move toward the DOCTOR. *A general stir.*

YOUNG WOMAN: What's it doing?

SON: Where is it going?

DOCTOR: I'd say it moved in my direction.

LADY: My God!

WIFE: And why did it move toward you?

FRIEND: What does it mean? That he's the person who's suffering most?

LADY: So it seems.

DOCTOR: Well, it had to be someone.

FRIEND: You see? I admit the game's getting interesting.

SON: I thought you didn't believe in it.

FRIEND: I don't but it's getting interesting.

LADY: Are there anymore questions?

FRIEND: The inevitable ones. We must find out why our esteemed doctor allows himself the luxury of suffering more than the rest of us.

SON: How do you expect the table to explain why someone suffers?

FRIEND: Your mother has said that the table always rises to the occasion.

DOCTOR: Now that I've been tapped, I won't object to continuing.

WIFE: (*To the* DOCTOR, *not at all uneasy.*) And why would you be suffering?

DOCTOR: I'm really not aware of suffering in any special way.

FRIEND: Shall we continue the game, then?

DOCTOR: By all means.

FRIEND: Your hands. (THEY *remake the circuit.*) I'll ask.

DOCTOR: And don't be afraid.

FRIEND: (*To the* LADY.) Can I ask?

LADY: Yes.

FRIEND: Table, you've told us which of us was suffering most. Now tell us why he's suffering. Is it because of professional problems?

Two taps.

LADY: No

FRIEND: Because of personal problems?

One tap.

LADY: Yes.

FRIEND: Is there any hatred in his suffering?

Two taps.

LADY: No.

SON: You really enjoy being morbid.

FRIEND: Be quiet. There's no hatred. (*Pause.*) Is there love?

One tap.

LADY: Yes.

FRIEND: Is love making him suffer?

One tap.

LADY: Yes.

FRIEND: Is he suffering because of his wife?

Two taps.

LADY: No.

WIFE: I'm glad it's not because of me.

SON: Let's stop now. We've heard enough, haven't we?

DOCTOR: Definitely not now. If it's not boring you too much, let's go on for my sake.

FRIEND: (*To the* SON.) You heard him! Be quiet and don't interrupt. The doctor is suffering over love, but he doesn't suffer because of his wife who is right here. (*Pause.*) Table, does the doctor have a lover?

The table hesitates. One tap and, immediately following it, another very feeble one.

SON: No. The table has answered no.

FRIEND: It tapped once, it answered yes.

LADY: Two times. The second was more timid, but two.

FRIEND: And why so timid?

LADY: The table knows what it's doing.

FRIEND: The table hesitated.

WIFE: (*Laughing.*) It's true, it did hesitate.

DOCTOR: I think it did, too. How curious. Either one has a lover or one doesn't.

YOUNG WOMAN: This is getting on my nerves. Do you want to continue?

SON: No, I don't.

DOCTOR: I'm sorry to have become the main attraction.

SON: Nobody wants to continue.

FRIEND: Let everyone speak for himself.

YOUNG WOMAN: Do you want to?

DOCTOR: It's all the same to me. If it's amusing you . . . (*To his* WIFE.) What do you say?

WIFE: It would be a shame to stop now, don't you think?

FRIEND: Those affected most give their approval. Bravo for them!

WIFE: Yes, go on with the questions.

FRIEND: A question for the table: If it's true that the doctor has a lover, can his suffering be due to the fact that she's stopped loving him?

Two taps.

LADY: (*Quickly.*) No.

WIFE: (*To the* FRIEND.) This time your morbid curiosity has failed you.

FRIEND: I'll grant that. Let's go back. Let's forget about the supposed lover. Let's see, we've agreed that he's suffering for personal reasons rather than professional ones. Let's secure the terrain. Is he suffering because of a specific person?

One tap.

LADY: Yes.

FRIEND: And it's not because of his wife. And we've ruled out a lover. Does he have parents?

Two taps.

LADY: No.

FRIEND: You don't?

DOCTOR: From my experience the table always tells the truth, if it can.

SON: As long as one of those present knows the truth.

DOCTOR: I don't have parents.

FRIEND: Well then, table, does he have children?

A much sharper tap than the previous ones.

YOUNG WOMAN: What is it, then?

LADY: It's a yes.

FRIEND: A special yes.

YOUNG WOMAN: A louder tap.

LADY: There's nothing gratuitous about it.

FRIEND: Children. Earlier you spoke about your daughter.

WIFE: Yes.

FRIEND: As I recall, your only child.

WIFE: Yes, you have a good memory.

FRIEND: Let the table speak. Let's see, table. The person among us who suffers most, is he suffering because of his daughter?

One tap.

LADY: Yes.

YOUNG WOMAN: Really.

FRIEND: Is the daughter sick?

Two taps.

LADY: No.

FRIEND: It's getting difficult.

SON: Give up, and let's move on to another topic.

FRIEND: Wait. Has the daughter done something the father doesn't like?

Two taps.

LADY: No. (*Suddenly.*) Ask the table if there is some way out for this suffering.

FRIEND: Do you see a solution for our friend's suffering?

One tap.

LADY: Yes.

FRIEND: An easy solution?

Two taps.

LADY: No. But will he be able to achieve the solution? (*One tap.*) Yes.

FRIEND: I want to know what the solution is. Everyone at peace, everyone contented, a happy ending . . .

Suddenly the table begins to tap with a rapid rhythm.

YOUNG WOMAN: Quiet! Who's counting?

SON: (*Referring to the* LADY.) She's doing it already.

In effect, the LADY *has begun to count the taps in a low voice.*

FRIEND: What's going on?

The table stops.

LADY: (*Aloud.*) Four!

WIFE: Four.

LADY: Continue.

The table begins to tap again, and the LADY *resumes counting in a low voice.*

FRIEND: Can you explain to me what this is all about?

SON: Be quiet!

DOCTOR: They're letters.

FRIEND: What?

YOUNG WOMAN: Wait!

LADY: (*When the table stops again.*) Five.

YOUNG WOMAN: (*Removing her hands from the circle to jot down the numbers.*) Four and five.

LADY: All right. Continue. (*The table taps only once and stops.*) Just one.

YOUNG WOMAN: One.

LADY: Continue.

The table begins again. The LADY *counts in a low voice.*

FRIEND: How long does this go on?

SON: It depends.

DOCTOR: The table is answering your question. With words. With letters that make words.

FRIEND: What do you mean?

The table stops.

LADY: Twenty.

YOUNG WOMAN: (*Jotting down.*) Twenty.

LADY: Continue.

The table starts again. The LADY *counts.*

FRIEND: Are they letters?

SON: Yes.

DOCTOR: Each series of taps indicate the place of a letter in the alphabet. Each group of letters will form a word. Get it?

FRIEND: I don't know. And then what?

WIFE: Then the answer to your question.

The table stops.

LADY: Eight.

YOUNG WOMAN: (*Jotting down.*) Eight.

LADY: Continue. (*The table remains still.*) Another, the letter that comes next. (*The table is still.*) Have you finished? (*One tap from the table.*)

WIFE: Is it over?

LADY: Yes.

FRIEND: So quickly?

DOCTOR: Let's see what it spells.

FRIEND: Are you sure it will be a word?

YOUNG WOMAN: You'll see now. (*To the* LADY.) Shall I count?

LADY: Let's see what we get.

The YOUNG WOMAN *counts on her fingers as* SHE *says the letters in a low voice.*

YOUNG WOMAN: The first letter, four. Four is a "D."

LADY: It begins with a "D."

YOUNG WOMAN: The second, five. An "E."

LADY: "E."

YOUNG WOMAN: The next is easy. One tap is "A."

LADY: "A."

YOUNG WOMAN: Twenty is . . . (*Counting softly as fast as* SHE *can.*) . . . "T."

LADY: "T."

YOUNG WOMAN: And the last is eight. An "H." D-E-A-T-H.

LADY: Death.

SON: How stupid.

FRIEND: How did you people do that?

LADY: It's always the table alone, believe me.

FRIEND: But how did you manage it?

SON: I don't want to play anymore.

DOCTOR: We all seem to be very impressed. (*To the* FRIEND.) And you, too.

SON: We can't draw any conclusions from this.

FRIEND: It's quite clear. We can conclude that death will solve the problem. (*To the* DOCTOR.) In fact, there's no problem that death doesn't solve.

WIFE: I, quite frankly, have enjoyed it a lot.

FRIEND: We should continue.

LADY: I'd forget about it.

SON: I don't know if you heard me. I refuse to continue. The rest of you can do as you please.

FRIEND: (*To the* LADY.) I'm sure that when you were children you didn't stop the moment it got interesting.

LADY: It varied.

FRIEND: You said that with the table order would return. Order hasn't returned yet.

LADY: Those were children's games.

FRIEND: We're children, too.

SON: (*Getting up.*) Who wants a drink?

YOUNG WOMAN: I'm getting hungry, what I'd like is dinner.

LADY: Then let's leave it for now.

WIFE: As you wish.

The LADY *gets up.*

FRIEND: A shameful retreat.

DOCTOR: The majority rules, we must surrender. (HE *also gets up and his* WIFE *with him.*) Besides, I really have to be going.

LADY: So soon?

DOCTOR: Yes, it's getting close to my appointment.

WIFE: Do you want me to go with you?

DOCTOR: Not at all. You'd be missed.

LADY: (*To the* WIFE.) Yes, do stay, please.

WIFE: I'll stay, I'll stay. (*To the* DOCTOR.) Then run along. I'll call you at home later.

DOCTOR: Don't. Well, if you do call and I'm still not home, you mustn't worry. I may go for a walk.

FRIEND: (*Who has heard them.*) So you prefer taking a stroll to our company?

WIFE: He needs the exercise.

DOCTOR: You've seen through me, haven't you? Goodbye, it's been great seeing you again. (*To the* LADY.) A kiss. And take care of my wife. (*To the others.*) Goodbye, everyone. Enjoy yourselves.

SON: I'll go with you to the door.

The DOCTOR *and the* SON *exit.*

FRIEND: He seems to be in a hurry.

YOUNG WOMAN: He wants to see his daughter.

FRIEND: So I heard.

WIFE: (*Calmly.*) Maybe it's not our daughter, maybe he's going to see his lover.

LADY: And you treat it as a joke!

WIFE: That lover from the table who may or may not exist. I certainly don't know. But if she does, he'll tell me. It will be a long explanation. I'll listen to it, and I'll die laughing, and he will suddenly feel a great tenderness for me. And I will have won. I'll confess that my husband holds no surprises for me.

Pause.

FRIEND: Pardon me.

The telephone rings. The LADY *answers it.*

LADY: Hello. Yes, yes, just a moment. (*To the* FRIEND.) It's for you.

YOUNG WOMAN: (*To the* LADY.) Shall we straighten things up a bit before dinner?

FRIEND: (*On the phone.*) Who is it? Oh, hello.

LADY: (*To the* YOUNG WOMAN.) No need.

FRIEND: (*On the phone.*) Yes?

YOUNG WOMAN: Only a little.

THEY *move aside and the* FRIEND *continues on the phone. The* SON *returns and assists the women.*

FRIEND: Yes? Fine, fine. Well, to be sure, it's a great relief. I'm happy. They had me sweating. Really? How do you know? Oh, all the better! Do you realize it's ten o'clock at night?

SON: (*Looking at his watch.*) Ten?

FRIEND: (*On the phone.*) I was beginning to resign myself. You'll have that dinner I promised. No need for the others to know yet. Where? Fine. What do you think of it? Thanks. You've gone to a lot of trouble. A dinner can hardly repay you. See you. (HE *hangs up.*)

SON: So?

FRIEND: They've given it to me.

LADY: What's happened?

SON: Congratulate him. Just as I expected, he's won. They've chosen his sculpture.

YOUNG WOMAN: Naturally, what else? Congratulations.

WIFE: I'm very happy for you. It's a great relief for us.

FRIEND: But, did you all know?

LADY: How could we not know?

SON: There's no way to keep certain things secret. Why do you think we put up with all your nastiness?

FRIEND: I didn't notice that you were being so tolerant.

SON: You don't say.

WIFE: What kind of sculpture is it?

FRIEND: Forms that interest me, it's hard to describe. I'm embarrassed to admit it but . . . it's going to have a name. Hold on tight, I'm going to call the sculpture "Time."

SON: Where's the champagne? There's something else we have to celebrate. Maybe less important, but that's beside the point. I was hoping it could be right on the hour, though on that occasion I wasn't paying much attention to the clock. (*To the* YOUNG WOMAN.) Here, for having put up with me for six years. (HE *hands her a gift.*)

YOUNG WOMAN: You remembered! I was certain you'd forgotten. Idiot! It's lovely, thank you so much. How nice!

LADY: You see? (*To the others.*) She was really quite depressed.

YOUNG WOMAN: Don't tell on me.

SON: Could that be why you were such a bad mood? Just over that?

YOUNG WOMAN: So? Yes, it was that.

SON: No other reason? Last year I gave you your gift at noon and you hinted that you would have preferred to get it at the exact hour.

YOUNG WOMAN: Really? Maybe I did.

FRIEND: End of the comedy of errors.

YOUNG WOMAN: Now my conscience is bothering me. I have to confess that I got even a bit. Earlier, I made a call on the other phone.

SON: Where did you call?

YOUNG WOMAN: Home. And I didn't tell you something because I was mad at you.

SON: How's the boy?

YOUNG WOMAN: Fine. His fever's completely gone.

LADY: Of course.

YOUNG WOMAN: Relieved?

SON: I'm glad you called.

LADY: Now you won't have to hurry off after dinner.

SON: I suppose not.

FRIEND: I'm in no hurry either. We can still make the table dance again, if you'd like.

SON: (*To the* LADY.) When the children come, you'll make it dance for them, just like your father made it dance for you and you for me.

LADY: And when will that be?

SON: Don't you want them to spend a few weeks with you?

LADY: Yes, but . . .

SON: What?

LADY: You didn't seem to be so sure about it.

SON: I thought it was settled. You didn't? You don't want them?

WIFE: She couldn't want anything more.

LADY: No need to make so much over it.

Pause.

WIFE: It's already night.

FRIEND: Yes.

LADY: Nights like this make me melancholy. But I love them.

SON: Now you're getting sentimental.

FRIEND: A little sentimentality, from time to time, isn't a bad thing.

SON: The perfect topic for a summer night.

YOUNG WOMAN: I'd like to have a lot more like this.

SON: You will.

Pause.

LADY: Everyone breathe deeply.

FRIEND: What?

LADY: Breathe deeply.

Pause.

YOUNG WOMAN: Like this.

Pause.

WIFE: (*Trivially.*) I was thinking . . . why do you suppose the table spelled out the word "death"?

Pause. Then LIGHTS DOWN.

ACT TWO

Vault of the sky. Wide, comfortable outdoor chairs.

Transparent night. A GIRL *of twenty-three seated and looking up and down at the sky. There is a folded blanket beside her. The* DOCTOR *enters from behind with his medical bag, which he immediately puts down. He approaches the* GIRL *slowly, passes his hand through her hair, leans over and kisses her head. The* GIRL *shows no surprise and does not turn around to see who it is.*

DOCTOR: Good evening.

GIRL: Hello.

DOCTOR: What are you doing?

GIRL: Besides looking at the sky?

DOCTOR: What are you looking for?

GIRL: A star, of course.

DOCTOR: How will you know that you've found it?

GIRL: A shooting star. When it passes, I'll have found it. What do you think, will I be lucky?

DOCTOR: It's the time of year for stars with tails. I've always called them stars with tails. But shooting star says it better.

GIRL: I'll see it for sure. I'll be satisfied with one. It's a very clear night. And there'll be a lot more. Did you realize that? I'll see many more. You know, on a night like this it seems like the world is being born, that the world is beginning. Does everyone feel that or just me? Do you feel it? The world is being born, it's mine. I can do with it what I please, what I please, anything.

DOCTOR: Yes, you are God, congratulations.

GIRL: Be quiet, you're too serious. I'll go where I want. I just hope a shooting
    star will pass by. Then I'll make a wish, I'll wish to fly like it flies, and
    the wish will come true. I'll fly up to one of those points of light.
    Goodbye.

Pause.

DOCTOR: Good evening, it's me. Just me. Can I come in?

GIRL: I'll fly, you know. (SHE *turns around for the first time and hugs him.*)

DOCTOR: Of course you'll fly. (HE *kisses her.*) I've left the others there.

GIRL: I wasn't looking at the sky.

DOCTOR: No?

GIRL: I mean I wasn't looking at the sky because it was the marvelous thing
    I could do tonight. I was looking at the sky because I was waiting for
    you. I wanted you to come. I wish you hadn't come.

DOCTOR: I had to bring you something.

GIRL: Where are they?

DOCTOR: I have them in the bag.

GIRL: Do you want me to take the first one?

DOCTOR: There's time.

GIRL: Will you remember?

DOCTOR: I'm a doctor.

GIRL: That doesn't mean anything. Maybe you won't want to remember.

DOCTOR: But I will. Why have you brought that blanket out?

GIRL: In case it turns chilly. I like blankets. They remind me of when my father used to tuck me in as a child. I'm lazy. I don't want to move. I was thinking . . . that at last I'll be able to fulfill a wish that's all mine. Not the wish I'd dreamed of, maybe not, but at least one I'll be capable of making come true. And that's not so bad, I'll have you know. Not so bad at all.

DOCTOR: I'm too serious, I agree, but you are so uncomplicated.

GIRL: I knew it, it embarrasses you to feel the way you do.

DOCTOR: Yes, it's hard for me to admit that I like your simplicity.

GIRL: You're lying.

DOCTOR: So what?

GIRL: Are we going to have an argument?

DOCTOR: We never really fight.

GIRL: I know how to deal with you. The experience of living. I'm old.

DOCTOR: Yes?

GIRL: I'm very old, I have a lot of experience and I have a stomach full of words I've had to swallow. Do you want me to tell you which ones? (*Pause.*) Then I won't tell you, and instead try to remember when you used to say to me, and you did, that swallowing words makes people old.

DOCTOR: I remember, I did say that. Of course you're old, I know it perfectly.

GIRL: You said too many things. Do you know how I discovered the summer skies? It's all your fault you've found me enthralled, waiting for a shooting star.

DOCTOR: That, too?

GIRL: You had given me a kaleidoscope. Aren't kaleidoscopes presents for children? You assured me, they're presents for people we love. And I thought: if he believes it . . . Afterwards, the kaleidoscope delighted me. For a change, you were right. I didn't want to learn that it was only a game with three pieces of glass, and I was filled with wonder over the changing forms and colors. The constant change. If you like a figure you see in a kaleidoscope, take a good look and say goodbye. You'll never find it again. You explained that to me, too. Move the kaleidoscope, an image dissolves and another is created as fleeting as the previous one. I don't know if you used the word fleeting. I never got tired of looking through the kaleidoscope. And one day you took it away from me. Last year, also at the start of summer. Also at night. You asked me to put down the kaleidoscope for a moment and to look up at the sky. To look at the other side of the coin. In the kaleidoscope everything changes. In the sky everything repeats itself. I looked and, as I'd always been an obedient daughter—no more, I'm sorry—I tried to understand you. You told me a few names of constellations that you knew and you kept repeating to me that we don't live under a friendly vault adorned with lighted bulbs, but under a bottomless hole, an empty space we don't understand. But you also said we shouldn't be afraid, that we should learn to let ourselves go. To let ourselves go as if we're up on a roller-coaster and see that we're about to plunge into the depths. If we become tense, it's awful, we'll have a bad time of it, but if we let ourselves go, then it's like being drunk. With the hole we have over us, the sky, it's just the same. Letting yourself go doesn't turn out to be so easy. The kaleidoscope is unpredictable, but it doesn't scare you; rather you learn to go from the kaleidoscope to the vault of the sky . . . But I've succeeded, you'll see. I'll fly. And don't protest, you were the one who pushed me. You put me at the summit. I'll make the kaleidoscope and sky one and the same.

DOCTOR: You talk and talk: words.

GIRL: There must be some way to erase the contradictions.

DOCTOR: There's no law, there are no contradictions, there's nothing. There's only letting yourself go.

GIRL: I can't stand you. Why do I put up with you when I can't stand you?

DOCTOR: Wait, the sight that works for you, now I know what it is. For me . . . the Universe, the black hole, yes, it's just fine! But I prefer to look at you. Your enthusiasm is the best sight I can imagine. Why don't I just look at you then, silently, instead of spoiling the party? I don't know.

SHE *touches him.*

GIRL: What are you afraid of?

DOCTOR: Let's see, what am I afraid of? For one thing, I'm afraid of . . . losing you.

GIRL: It doesn't seem that way.

DOCTOR: Do I hide it well?

GIRL: Too well.

DOCTOR: But I'm about to lose you.

GIRL: It still depends on you.

DOCTOR: I won't lose you.

GIRL: (*Hard.*) But you've never had me.

DOCTOR: The things you say. (*Change.*) Are you sure you'll need the blanket?

GIRL: It could turn cool. And I don't want to go back inside all night. Here, like this, all night.

DOCTOR: And if I make you go in?

GIRL: You can't.

DOCTOR: A sweater would be more comfortable than a blanket.

GIRL: I like to wrap myself in a blanket. I'll tell you again: it reminds me of when my father tucked me in bed as a child.

Pause.

DOCTOR: Really? Is that the reason?

Long pause.

GIRL: Daddy.

DOCTOR: Yes. Is that the reason?

GIRL: When you used to tuck me in.

DOCTOR: I liked to tuck you in.

GIRL: Why did you come so early?

DOCTOR: You can imagine.

GIRL: I don't like goodbyes.

DOCTOR: I also had to go over some papers. (*Pause.*) A lie.

GIRL: You don't know how to deal with my leaving.

DOCTOR: What do you mean I don't? It's fine that you're going, it's very fine
that you're going. You'll fly. Isn't flying what it's about, jumping into the
emptiness? So, come, fly away. You'll meet people, you'll get to know
new places, live stories that I've never lived . . . Fabulous, perfect,
fantastic, you don't know what a mess you're getting yourself into. I
can't understand at all why you're going. Why are you going? I do
understand why you're going, it's obvious that I understand why you're
going. And you think I'm the kind of father who turns my stomach as
much as he does yours? I'm a different kind of father. But not different
in the way you think. (HE *feels a shiver.*) Oh, my God.

GIRL: I'll spare you the shame of describing the spectacle I have before me.

DOCTOR: It won't be of any use to you to go. I wish it would be, and I'd
bite my tongue and I'd think: fine. But it won't be of any use to you.

GIRL: Either you're deceiving me or you're mistaken. It will be of use to me.

DOCTOR: There's no need to go.

GIRL: Didn't you just say that you understand perfectly why I'm going? I don't have to explain anything to you. So relax, it's nothing. You don't want me to do it, what you want is to talk and talk, and all the while you're annoying me as much as you can, I suppose to ruin my last night. That's enough, father!

DOCTOR: (*Change.*) Do you have . . . ? Do you have everything ready?

GIRL: Why don't you go back? They'll be happy to see you again.

DOCTOR: Thank you.

GIRL: Go back, leave me alone, don't ruin it for me. I'm doing the right thing to go.

DOCTOR: Daughter . . .

GIRL: (*Change of tone.*) No. Stay.

DOCTOR: I won't move.

GIRL: We'll talk like two old friends until dawn. We won't go to sleep: we won't sleep a wink all night.

DOCTOR: A few more hours with my daughter.

GIRL: Oh, don't forget about the pills.

DOCTOR: The pills. Maybe we won't use them.

GIRL: I need them for the trip. I don't want to catch a fever or microbes or things like that. What is it, then? Blackmail?

DOCTOR: Don't worry: you won't lack anything that can make your trip more comfortable. Can you imagine that your father would deny you anything?

GIRL: Sometimes I don't trust you.

DOCTOR: I only want to help you. I'll help you no matter what. Once, when you were little . . .

GIRL: Tell me things about when I was little.

DOCTOR: You had a lot of sore throats, a stuffed up nose, your breathing was bad, you'd get nervous, you were sleepy but the mucus and the discomfort kept you awake, you would fret without really crying, and you were a lot of trouble. You were about five then. Your mother wanted to care for you, but I didn't let her. I sat on your bed, I picked you up, and you looked at me with those sad, half-asleep eyes, you complained, and I said ssshhh, that everything would be all right, while I held you resting on my chest. That way you could breathe better. And feeling yourself with me, you could relax. You fell asleep and I stayed on, sitting in the dark, and I rocked you from time to time until daybreak. First I thought: damn these childhood illnesses; when I left I felt a sweet peacefulness, a peacefulness . . . I'll always help you, I'll always love you. (*Pause.*) The problem . . . No, problem, no. The . . . question. There's a question . . . the way that I love you. (*Pause.*) I'll add nothing more except in the presence of my attorney. Have you taken out the garbage?

GIRL: You've just said it. You've admitted it.

DOCTOR: Of course you haven't taken it out. I'll go look for the bags.

Exits. The GIRL*, alone, speaks loudly.*

GIRL: You've admitted it. Don't come back right away. I want to talk, now I do, and I want you to hear me, but I don't want to see you while I'm talking. You've told me a memory of the past, a real, authentic memory. Now I want to tell you one of a time that is yet to come. We can't know what will happen, over a period of time, and surely what I'm going to tell you won't happen. I'll tell you a lie. Don't come back, wait. Be patient and wait until I've finished. A special memory: mother will have died, let's imagine it. Don't move. You won't move, right? If mother died . . . I don't want her to die. If mother died, we'd cry. We'd find ourselves terribly alone. We'd buy, we will buy a wreath of carnations, not just any wreath, a huge wreath, the largest we can find, because she liked carnations, and we'll place it on her casket. It won't be of any use, it'll be a useless gesture. Then I'll insist that they cremate her and you'll say yes, whatever I want, and they'll cremate her and in that way her body will go from being sweet and welcoming to a handful of remains and dust, without the shame of decay. We'll scatter her ashes in the sea. It's where people scatter ashes when they don't know what to do with them and they don't have a more original idea. We'll scatter them in the sea, at night, perhaps, a sad night because we feel sad. A night, for example, like this one. Afterwards . . . Afterwards you won't be seeing any other woman. You'll preserve mother's memory, you'll be an eternally faithful widower. People will say: that man overdoes it. Some of them will laugh behind your back, and others, in contrast, will admire the strength of your decision. I'll stay here. I won't go away. I'll take care of you. Forever. A sacrificing daughter, who will waste her life in a senseless way. (*Pause.*) I've finished. (*Pause. The* DOCTOR *enters with a roll of plastic garbage bags which he quickly puts down any place.*)

DOCTOR: Fine, done.

GIRL: And so?

DOCTOR: What?

GIRL: Did you like it?

DOCTOR: Here are the bags.

GIRL: Did you like my memory?

DOCTOR: What are you talking about?

GIRL: You're faking.

DOCTOR: I'll leave them in sight to remind me to use them.

GIRL: Lying coward.

DOCTOR: Don't get excited. Yes, I heard you. So?

GIRL: If nothing better occurs to you, you could say, for example, that I and my sick, make-believe memories disgust you.

DOCTOR: I won't say it. You shouldn't give so much importance to your feelings. Or to mine either. Our story has no importance at all.

GIRL: You've spoiled the night.

DOCTOR: I couldn't help it. You want to leave tomorrow.

GIRL: Well, yes, put it any way you want, tomorrow I'll set out on a long trip, and it won't end with a return home. It'll end some other place. Mother and you know it but you don't want to admit it to yourselves: I'll not come back. I'll stop some place no better than this, I have no illusions about it, but it won't be here. And do you know where it will begin? On a blue, green, orange island, where I'll make love as the sun sets. A saccharine moment, and many others are yet to come . . . , as many as I can find. To remember them and savor them later, when the trip is over.

DOCTOR: A splendid trip and a girl who knows how to dream—you think you're unhappy but you don't stop dreaming—her adventure will begin making love as the sun sets.

GIRL: Yes. And as she makes love she will think of her father.

DOCTOR: . . .

GIRL: I'll make love and I'll think of my father. What do you think, is there any remedy?

DOCTOR: Time, if it's worth waiting for time to pass.

GIRL: I'm going. I'm dying to go. Don't look at me that way, stupid. Why are you looking at me that way?

Pause.

DOCTOR: I've admitted it, indeed I have. No woman had ever bound me;

never this unhealthy, troubling sensation until you appeared. But that's not really the problem. Our relationship has no importance, it's routine. A man of a certain age who desires a young girl and a young girl who is dazzled by a man of a certain age. Whether we have the same blood or not, it's a detail that concerns no one. The question is something else, but let's forget it. At least for a few moments, let's forget it.

GIRL: Go on.

DOCTOR: You're my child, my only daughter, the woman who came from my seed, from my hands and my words. Nothing can be closer to me. If you aren't mine, nothing is mine in this world. You are completely mine, beyond debate, above any sense of modesty, just as the most elemental laws of nature, the most comic, the most ridiculous laws of nature dictate it. And you will be mine, come what may, no matter where you go, no matter whom you're with, even on the day you've stopped remembering me. Don't speak, I'm talking, until the day you've stopped remembering me. You think it's impossible to forget me, but you will, of course you will. And all the same you'll go on being mine. No one or any thing can erase it, not even you: you are my daughter and for exactly that reason I love you with a strength greater than a man has to love a woman. No one could love you as I do, or with such intensity or such clarity. That's why I'll know, like no one else, how to protect you from horror. I'll protect you from horror with the fury that I clutched you to my chest that night, when you were a child. Have you understood? What more is there? Have I said what you wanted?

GIRL: Almost.

DOCTOR: Surely I have, or you haven't understood me.

GIRL: You've said what I wanted, but don't stop.

DOCTOR: I've used up my words.

GIRL: No, words, no.

DOCTOR: You said don't stop . . .

GIRL: Come.

DOCTOR: Remember, I'll protect you from horror.

GIRL: You can't stop now.

DOCTOR: I'll protect you from it.

GIRL: Stop talking. (SHE *picks up the blanket, unfolds it, and spreads it on the
ground. SHE looks at her father. SHE begins to remove her clothes without
embarrassment, innocently. When SHE is half-undressed, the DOCTOR moves
closer to her, helps her with a button to remove some article of clothing, just as he
would do for a child. Then HE embraces her tenderly. SHE clutches him
passionately. In an embrace, they kneel on the blanket. Slowly they lie on the blanket,
the GIRL beneath the DOCTOR. HE kisses different parts of her body gently,
until HE reaches her mouth. SHE holds him and intensifies the kiss. Afterwards,
SHE moves away a bit and laughs.*) Father! (SHE *unfastens his clothes, they roll
on the blanket, we hear a soft moan, a hand takes a corner of the blanket and, with
a single broad gesture, covers the two bodies. Movements under the blanket. And,
suddenly, calm.*)

Pause. The blanket opens suddenly. We see the DOCTOR *and the* GIRL *again, half-
nude, lying relaxed.*

GIRL: The stars have moved in the sky.

Pause. A telephone rings. SHE *starts to get up to answer it.*

DOCTOR: No. (HE *draws her back and embraces her.*)

GIRL: Get up and straighten your clothes. (*They get up.*)

DOCTOR: We have to think about the pills.

GIRL: I'm not going on a trip. Come here, let me fix you.

DOCTOR: Do what you want.

GIRL: Are you worried?

DOCTOR: No.

The GIRL *has arranged his clothes for him.*

GIRL: Fine. Now you look better.

DOCTOR: (*Tenderly.*) You seem like a married woman brushing the lint off her husband to show him off to friends.

GIRL: I'm not a married woman. We're two clandestine lovers. And we have to get used to exchanging secrets. We'll look for a safe place. An apartment where we can scream and laugh and let ourselves go . . . Of course, a daughter can walk down the street on her father's arm.

DOCTOR: You're radiant because of me.

GIRL: A father can put his hand on his daughter's cheek. I'm radiant because of you, yes. The world is being born, it's mine. No thanks to a trip that will end far from here, but at your side. Sighting a falling star would round off the night.

DOCTOR: You'll see one.

GIRL: I've got to resolve the mess about the trip. I'll invent an excuse. I'll lie shamelessly. But I'll wait until the last minute, tonight I don't want to worry about anything. I only want to watch the sky with you beside me.

DOCTOR: What sky? Thousands and thousands of stars that are sending a final sign of their dying light. A sight that quickly degenerates into a cheap lyric. Millions and millions of enormous bodies which whirl endlessly, a frenetic movement, an excessive waste of energy that's consumed uselessly.

GIRL: But it's nice to look at.

DOCTOR: Do you enjoy looking at something that's meaningless?

GIRL: The apartment would have to be small, one bedroom, bath, kitchen . . .

DOCTOR: Energy that's wasted, frenetic spasm after frenetic spasm in a black hole.

GIRL: I'll take charge of looking for it.

DOCTOR: The Universe is no enigma at all. Its indecent contractions and expansions are only a display. It's one big stupidity.

GIRL: The neighborhood, we have to decide which neighborhood. It has to be far from home.

DOCTOR: The sky's absolute idiocy. A stupidity that inspires stupor, nostalgia, wonder, secret hopes . . . Looking at the vault above us, we collect I don't know what kind of secret hopes.

GIRL: Have you finished?

DOCTOR: If it doesn't interest you, yes.

GIRL: You don't have to talk if you don't want to. I'll speak for both of us.

DOCTOR: You won't speak for me.

GIRL: Sometimes we have to look for a way . . . A few days together. You pretend you're going some place or other, and so will I. Each for a different reason. No, wait. I'll get sick. A long illness that will require a lot of care. You'll recommend a stay at a pleasant place to rest. And you feel obliged to visit me often. Alone. How does that strike you?

DOCTOR: An imaginary illness. For once you don't have to struggle in vain against pain, a failing body and death. A failing body and death are inevitable. Pain, maybe . . .

GIRL: That's enough. You're annoying me. You're doing it on purpose. Enough. Why are you doing it?

DOCTOR: I'm trying to gain time.

GIRL: Are you bored?

DOCTOR: I wouldn't want time to end. (*A telephone rings. The* DOCTOR *and the* GIRL *look at each other in silence, at a certain distance, with slight seriousness. Perhaps* SHE *ends up averting her eyes. The phone stops ringing.*) I would like to explain so many things to you before time ends. For example, that living is painful. And that trying to erase our pain only serves to cause pain in others.

GIRL: I'm not hurting anyone.

DOCTOR: We can't help hurting others.

GIRL: You're hurting me. You'll be sorry.

DOCTOR: Let me speak.

GIRL: You'll be sorry. It's disgusting, you'll be sorry.

DOCTOR: You have been an unbearable weight on me from the day you were born. I didn't want you to be born. I didn't want children. But women always end up deciding and your mother decided to have you.

GIRL: What are you saying?

DOCTOR: A child is a bother one is never free of again. Being responsible for you, for your health, for bringing you up, and for your future . . . your future . . . , a lot of senseless pain. I wish you hadn't been born, I wish I'd been spared the obsession of seeing you before me always, I wish I could have washed my hands of you, forgotten you, freed myself. But no, I have you here, in front of me, confused, entirely at my mercy. No, I won't do anything without thinking of you. Whatever I do, I'll do it for you. To the very end.

GIRL: Why are you telling me?

DOCTOR: Sit down here, with me, and make yourself look with my eyes. One after another, waves of pain strike us as we send out endless waves of pain to other people. The worst thing is that nobody wins, it has no more meaning than those ridiculous spasms of the stars. Do you understand? Do you see? At home or far away, it's the same, it'll always be the same. I've deceived you, there's no difference between the kaleidoscope and the vault of the sky; now you know the law that unites them: neither of them has any purpose. (*Pause.*) It's hard to put the blame on you, but don't worry, I don't intend to let you go.

GIRL: I'm tired. I can't do anything else, I can't. Please, let me go.

DOCTOR: I've finished. (*Tense pause.*) Are you thirsty? Do you want something to drink?

GIRL: Yes. (*The* DOCTOR *exits. The* GIRL *is alone.*) Black hole. A burden. Pain. I don't cause you any pain. (*Loudly.*) Father, where did you hide the kaleidoscope? (*Pause. Suddenly* SHE *lets out an anguished cry. The* DOCTOR *reappears with glasses and drinks.*) I've always been a burden, a bother! A father is only a poor guy full of good intentions. Other fathers; all except you. When there was a problem you always came and you fixed it, you always fixed everything. A hug, a few comforting words. My best friend . . . How did you do it? How did you know how to hide your disgust so well? Now you suddenly change your mind and I'm supposed to believe that you're my enemy. What have I done? Why did it happen? Why are you abandoning me? You never abandoned me. And I didn't get it. Pig. Why are you doing it? You son of a bitch! I'll go. I don't want to see you. I'll go. I'll make a call and I'll go at once. Don't touch me! Leave!

DOCTOR: Calm down!

GIRL: Get out of my sight, get out of my way, and let me pass!

DOCTOR: Will you be quiet? Don't go!

GIRL: I'm going! And I won't come back, I won't come back!

DOCTOR: Don't you move!

GIRL: I don't intend to stay a minute more!

DOCTOR: (*Hard and precise.*) I'm telling you not to go, don't go! Understand? (*Pause. Softly but firmly.*) Don't go. It's over. Order will return.

GIRL: I don't need you. You've said some frightening things. Why? And why today? Why, if you don't feel sorry. I'm just in the way.

DOCTOR: I won't fail you. I'm your father, I'm your doctor and, you'll see, I'll cure your pain. I've caused it and I'll take it away. I know what I'm saying. The pain will disappear, I promise. I'm the person who solved your problems. Yes, I'm glad you said that. You cried out for me at night, frightened; you thought you saw demons. I would get up, come to you, and the demons would disappear. The time you slept for hours against my chest I decided never to let the world hurt you, or allow the demons to do you harm. Don't be angry with me. It's night, and maybe I've invented demons to feel the way I did then. The world is being born, it's yours.

GIRL: I don't need you. I would have gone. I wouldn't have needed you.

DOCTOR: I know.

GIRL: But . . .

DOCTOR: But you're staying.

GIRL: Maybe. For your sake.

DOCTOR: But you don't need me.

GIRL: Yes I do. Always. What else do you want me to say?

DOCTOR: You'll stay with me. (*Pause. Easing of tension.*) Now let's talk about the pills.

GIRL: What pills?

DOCTOR: I know you aren't going on a trip now, but you're overexcited because of me. They'll relax you. (HE *picks up his bag and opens it. The* GIRL *goes to his side and sneaks a look. The* DOCTOR *takes out the container of pills that* HE *had taken out of the bag at the beginning of the first act.*)

GIRL: Are those the ones?

DOCTOR: Yes.

The GIRL puts her hand in the bag and takes out a little box.

GIRL: And this?

DOCTOR: Leave that alone.

GIRL: What is it?

DOCTOR: Something that has to be injected. Put it back. (HE *takes if from her.*)

GIRL: There's nothing else inside.

DOCTOR: You shouldn't ever touch a doctor's bag.

GIRL: There's no other medicine.

DOCTOR: Maybe not.

GIRL: And the pills for the trip?

DOCTOR: What?

GIRL: When you arrived you said you had the pills for the trip in your bag.

DOCTOR: Are you sure?

GIRL: Certain.

DOCTOR: Here. Take two.

GIRL: What will they do to me?

DOCTOR: They're tranquilizers. They'll make you feel relaxed. A little sleepy, maybe.

GIRL: Do I take them now?

Pause.

DOCTOR: Yes.

The GIRL *swallows them and then takes a few sips.*

GIRL: Done.

DOCTOR: Not yet.

GIRL: No?

DOCTOR: Now you have to get comfortable. Sit here.

GIRL: And you sit beside me.

The DOCTOR *sits beside her.*

DOCTOR: Let's talk a bit more. All right?

GIRL: Fine.

DOCTOR: Will you forgive me for the time I put you through?

GIRL: I'll forgive you for the painful part. Not the good. (*Pause.*) Let's talk.

DOCTOR: I really don't know why I complicate things so much.

GIRL: You enjoy it.

DOCTOR: Maybe we're getting close to some place, maybe the brilliance of the stars . . . Maybe, who knows, maybe they're a sign of friendship, of consolation . . .

GIRL: What do you want to tell me?

DOCTOR: Maybe each drop of horror will be repaid, someday, in some form, I don't know how, with a drop of pleasure.

GIRL: I think the pills are beginning to take effect.

DOCTOR: A drop of pleasure for every drop of horror. Possibly.

GIRL: I'm getting sleepy.

DOCTOR: What kind of sleepiness?

GIRL: Pleasant, sweet. But I don't know if I want to go to sleep.

DOCTOR: As you wish. Why not? You can sleep a while. I'll wake you up.

GIRL: But don't leave. Stay beside me while I sleep.

DOCTOR: I won't move.

GIRL: You'll play a trick on me. I know you.

DOCTOR: No, I promise. A father's word. Want me to hold your hand?

GIRL: No need.

DOCTOR: You aren't leaving me?

SHE *smiles and holds out her hand to him.* HE *takes it.*

GIRL: (*After closing her eyes.*) Keep on talking. Don't stop.

DOCTOR: Yes. What was I saying? That we know nothing. But that someday our experience will have meaning. Maybe it has already. Fears will vanish. There'll be a justification. It'll all become simple, easy and clear.

GIRL: (*With her eyes closed.*) Afterwards . . .

DOCTOR: What?

GIRL: Afterwards . . .

DOCTOR: Tell me.

GIRL: It's all the same. Remind me that afterwards . . . I have to tell you something.

DOCTOR: I'll remind you. (*Pause. Softly.*) I was really telling you a story with a happy ending. Simple, easy and clear. Do you want me to go on? What else? Stories have to be told well. I'll start at the beginning. Once there was a father and a daughter who were very close, very close. They lived in a warm and pleasant cabin, and outside there was a storm and wolves. The father said, no storm or wolves will ever get you; and I'm going to give you a gift that's almost magic so that they'll never harm you. (*Stops.*) Are you asleep? (HE *checks to see, kisses her on the cheek, and steps away.* HE *goes to his bag;* HE *finds the box with the injectable fluid and a syringe.* HE *fills the syringe. Meanwhile,* HE *hasn't stopped talking.*) What will you give me, the child asked. Will you give me a witch's broom and I'll go flying up the chimney and rise to the clouds and I'll have sunshine whenever I wish? No, I can't give you that. I don't have a witch's broom. Will you give me a magic wand so that I can turn wolves into lambs and we'll all be friends and we'll romp and play together? No, I can't give you that. I don't have a magic wand. Will you give me a cape that will make me invisible when I put it on and no one will see me and no one can harm me? No, I can't, I have no cape like that. But you're getting warm, you're very close (*The* DOCTOR *has completed his task.* HE *takes the syringe in one hand.* HE *goes to the girl, takes her arm and looks for a vein.*) With my almost magical gift there'll be no storm or wolves, and in fact you will become invisible. (*Pause.*) Since you are my daughter, I'll give you the best gift you can offer to anyone. I'll give you rest. Forever. (HE *pricks the* GIRL's *arm and inserts the hypodermic needle.*) It will be simple, easy and clear, you won't feel anything. (HE *withdraws the needle.*) Nothing. (HE *puts her arm down, goes to deposit the syringe, and returns to the* GIRL's *side.* HE *looks at her silently.* HE *takes her pulse. Pause.*) It's done. (HE *takes a deep breath.*) I didn't play a trick on you. I won't leave you. (HE *picks up the blanket, goes to look for a garbage bag, and carrying both things* HE *returns to the* GIRL's *side, sits beside her, covers her legs and his with the blanket, puts an arm around the girl, leans over and kisses her on the mouth.*) It's done. (HE *puts his head into the plastic garbage bag.* HE *fastens it tightly around his neck.* HE *takes one end of the blanket and with a broad, clean movement* HE *covers his own body and the* GIRL's*. Suddenly, through the firmament, a shooting star streaks by.*)

LIGHTS DOWN

ACT THREE

The same interior as Act One.

Night. The LADY, *the* SON, *the* YOUNG WOMAN, *the* FRIEND *and the* WIFE *are seated in relaxed attitudes, separated from one another.* THEY *are talking among themselves calmly, at times leaving long pauses.*

SON: Dinner was excellent, and we all agree about that. Don't protest anymore, Mama; they'll think you're fishing for compliments.

LADY: You're not being very nice to me.

YOUNG WOMAN: Really, everything was done to perfection.

FRIEND: As for me, I feel very much at home here.

WIFE: Shall we play the game with the table again?

LADY: Whenever the rest of you wish.

WIFE: Not yet. Just a moment, please.

SHE *gets up, goes to the phone, dials a number, listens.*

YOUNG WOMAN: Sometimes, quite suddenly, there's a special moment with friends, when you least expect it. You don't want it ever to end. You don't know how it began but it should last for an eternity. It's a moment, how shall I say, of harmony. And it comes from a bond of affection. We'd be embarrassed to say so. It doesn't matter. Affection is what it is. As for me, at this hour, after drinking more than I usually do, it's easy to say, for me there's nothing comparable to honest affection. Forgive me, I'm boring you.

The WIFE *hangs up and returns to her seat. The* LADY *gives her a questioning look.*

WIFE: (*Smiling.*) Nobody answers. I'll try again later. If you wish we can sit around the table.

No one moves. Pause.

YOUNG WOMAN: Affection, passion, love, desire . . . all that. What could
be more important? For me it's very clear. I don't pretend it's the same
for everyone else, I'm only speaking of my own experience. The bond
with the one you love. I can't understand life if it's not centered on that.
Oh, really, I don't know why you let me go on like this.

SON: (*Gently.*) But you're doing fine, talk on.

YOUNG WOMAN: (*Looking at him.*) Yes . . . ? Physical passion; it can't exist
without loving. For me, this relationship with another person gives life
its meaning. I'm rambling and maybe I'm totally wrong. I shouldn't
generalize but it's hard for me not to. I'm speaking of myself, all right,
only of myself. (*Pause.*) Only of myself? Physical passion can come to
be everything, and then comes the fear of possibly losing the other
person, the hurt of misunderstandings, suspicions . . . and jealousy, too.
You're unprotected, anyone who comes along can make you look
foolish. So what? Passion for another, yes. I hope it never ends.

Pause.

FRIEND: I don't give myself completely when I love. Do the rest of you give
yourselves totally when you love? Be honest.

LADY: I'll go bring more coffee. If anyone prefers herb tea, just say so.

SON: We'll be going after a while. What's the hurry?

WIFE: There's no rush.

YOUNG WOMAN: (*To the* FRIEND.) What were you saying?

FRIEND: Oh, I don't know. I'm not sure. (*Pause.*) That love, for me, is
something quick, that passes without leaving a trace. It must be some
deficiency in me, some piece of me that's always been broken. But, to
compensate—I don't know if it's to compensate—I have the objects
that leap from my fingers. My sculptures, you know. I don't mean that
those creations make me better than anyone else. But sometimes, when

I'm working against the tensions of metal or stone, time stops. It's usually at night, like now. I'm all alone with the material I'm forming. I don't want to bore you with this. Those forms that will end up resisting the rain and wind on the sparse grass of a city garden, or will stand in a corner of some house, useful because someone will rest their eyes on them . . . I won't be there anymore. What more can I do? I believe in that. For me there's nothing more. (*Pause.*) Shall we make the table dance?

LADY: So what do you think about the table, then? That it's a game? Maybe it is, but there's no trick about it. Don't tell me again that you're going to discover the trick. You'll make me angry. No, don't do that. Only a game, why not? Surely I don't seem ridiculous to you, with all the faith I put in it, the way I perceive it.

FRIEND: No, no. I won't say it again. I promise.

LADY: I can't help looking at the table with different eyes than yours. I believe in God, you see? There's nothing that ends, and all around me I see his signs. When I discover one of those signs, from time to time, my heart skips a beat. Signs that call out to us, that warn us and give us courage. I respect the ideas of other people, of course I do, but my own ideas make me feel safe, they help me believe that come what may we'll be happy again, in some way I can't explain, but I do know when . . . afterwards. Finding yourself at peace maybe . . . having some loving person close by, but above all, though I don't have that loving person, though it's hard for me to accept that loving person is missing in my life, in any case love will be there. I know that right now, together, we are at peace. We are, aren't we? I hope so, don't disappoint me. (*Pause.*) Right now we are at peace but it's only a sign that someday we'll find greater peace, forever. All of us here and those who are absent. All our absent ones, without exception.

The WIFE *gets up, goes to the telephone, dials a number and waits. The* OTHERS *are silent, calm. Pause. The* WIFE *hangs up and returns to her place.*

SON: The children . . . for example.

LADY: (*To the* FRIEND.) Thank you for coming.

FRIEND: I don't intend to leave until you throw me out.

LADY: Careful, you may stay here forever.

FRIEND: I think not, but it's a pity.

SON: There are also the children. No matter how peaceful I feel in any place, I wouldn't be able to stay there without my children. Now I know that they're at home, that they're safe, and the older boy's fever is gone, so I don't need to . . . (*To the* YOUNG WOMAN.) Better I shut up now, right?

YOUNG WOMAN: (*To the* OTHERS.) Sometimes he makes me feel jealous of my own children. (*To the* SON.) It's my fault, as if I didn't know you too well.

SON: Our relationship is important, of course. You and I, the way we understand each other when we talk, the way we understand each other in any situation. But, in the end, children transcend it all. (*To the* OTHERS.) We've argued about this I don't know how often, and we never agree.

YOUNG WOMAN: You can say it as often as you please but don't expect me to agree.

SON: (*To the* MOTHER.) I don't know anything about God. (*To the* FRIEND.) Objects can be truly beautiful, but they're still objects. Children . . . only with children do we have the possibility of something beyond all that. Learning to love a child, from the time he's born . . . to hold him in your arms when he's hurt and crying . . . He has absolute trust in you, he knows that you're the only one who will never harm him. He depends on you completely. And, of course, we'll die and our children will still be here. There's no consolation like that, to know that I shall die but a part of my memory will continue in my children. Don't think I'm trying to be profound, but the lives of my children takes precedence over mine. (*Pause.*) Well, what do we do now?

FRIEND: Nothing. The fact is I have to get up early tomorrow. The phone's not going to stop ringing, I can be sure of that. But now I'm in no hurry to leave. We still have to make the table dance again.

LADY: I'm glad you all came. It's been a long time since I've enjoyed myself so much.

SON: We realize that. No need to say more.

Suddenly the YOUNG WOMAN *goes to the side of the* LADY, *kisses her on the forehead, and stays beside her. The* SON *takes a bottle and pours a glass of water for himself. The* FRIEND *stretches out languorously, with no self-consciousness. Then* THEY *are all silent.*

WIFE: Tomorrow I, too, will have to get up early. All the bustle because my daughter's going away on a trip . . . If I don't help her pack, who knows what she's likely to forget. And my husband will have already left for work, but not before he's been a total nuisance. First getting him off, and then saying goodbye to her . . . then I'll be alone. I'll wash my hair. The shampoo will give my head a nice smell. I'll get the dryer. I'll settle in with a good novel in front of me., with one hand I'll pass the dryer over my hair and with the other I'll brush it, thoroughly, so thoroughly . . . As my hair dries, I'll bury myself in a story of crime and passion. I always try to make it last. Then I'll get dressed and look at the list of things I have to do. I've made a list of things, my agenda. Oh yes, tomorrow without fail, I have to call a painter; they've told me he's not expensive and that his work is very professional. I'm talking about an inside painter. He has to repaint the kitchen for me, to make it brighter. I hope he won't take his time giving me an estimate. Tomorrow the cleaning woman will arrive late. I make the best of it. Since she only comes two days a week, I busy myself with trivial things when she's there. Can you imagine me going to yoga classes? I only go once a week, I don't think it does me any good, but it's a distraction. For sure, tomorrow will be the last class, vacation is beginning. I must buy myself a summer blouse, I have to go window shopping. And a bathing suit, especially a bathing suit. I don't know why it excites me so much to talk of vacation. Vacations are for other people. I've worked very little outside the house. There was never anything I was good at. But I'm not bored. I've never been bored. For me just drying and brushing my hair is a pleasure. Daily tasks, trying to keep the house from falling apart, the hours I spend in the office, it all keeps my mind occupied. I like the routine of it. Things you do by routine. A little sense of humor and getting on with life. My daughter is grown up now, my love life is habit, my inventions are cooking recipes. And God is the nativity scene I put out at Christmas. Tomorrow I don't know what awaits me. The same as always. And what do you want me to tell you? Yes, I'm certain I don't need anything more in life. For me that amounts to happiness. My happiness. I don't expect anything more. (*Pause.*) I am truly happy.

Long pause. Suddenly the LADY *points upward, excited.*

LADY: Look quick, don't you see it? (THEY *all look in the direction* SHE *is pointing.*) A shooting star.

LIGHTS DOWN

Montserrat Esteve and Marta Angelat in *E.R.* (*Stages*),
Teatre Lliure (1994), directed by Josep Montanyès.
Photo: courtesy of the playwright

Marta Angelat, Maife Gil, and Mercè Aràguena in *E.R.*
(*Stages*), Teatre Lliure (1994), directed by Josep Montanyès.
Photo: courtesy of the playwright

STAGES

A Play in Six Scenes by

Josep M. Benet i Jornet

Translated by
Marion Peter Holt

CHARACTERS

The Girl

Gloria Marc

Angela Roca

Maria Caminal

SCENE ONE

Dark stage. An ovation erupts. Fervent applause and insistent enthusiastic bravos, which continue, fade, and disappear. Silence. Lights up on a small area of the stage, allowing us to see the GIRL.

GIRL: When I was a child, they gave me a little toy theatre. It was old and second hand, with a set and some cardboard figures that represented the characters. I spent hours playing with it. Whole days, without ever getting bored. One morning I took it to school with me and, I don't know exactly how, the other children destroyed all my little cardboard characters. And I couldn't play any more.

The lights come up on the entire space. We see a proscenium arch painted blue and gold. The stage is bare and has an abandoned look. At the moment there are no sets—except, perhaps, for an ostentatious curtain, half-drawn, at one side. A mature and still attractive woman, dressed practically but elegantly, starts to cross the stage with a sure, quick step.

GLORIA: (SHE *stops for a moment, turns back toward the side where* SHE *has just entered, and speaks loudly in a cold voice.*) The spotlight has got to hit me four seconds earlier. Is that clear? Tomorrow the curtain doesn't go up until we've tried it and you've got it right. (*Suddenly warm.*) I love you all! Good night, everyone. (SHE *continues her cross until the* GIRL *abruptly steps in her way.*)

GIRL: Excuse me, Miss Marc.

GLORIA: (*Smiling aloofly.*) Yes.

GIRL: Could you give me a moment of your time?

GLORIA: Who let you in here?

GIRL: I would like to speak with you for a moment.

GLORIA: What is it? Do you want my autograph?

GIRL: No.

GLORIA: That's a relief! At least you're original. Didn't you like my performance? Or maybe you didn't see it.

GIRL: Oh, yes, I saw it. Gloria Marc is the most important actress on the stage today. The best since Empar Ribera.

GLORIA: That good? How would you know? Empar Ribera died before you were born.

GIRL: But you knew her, right? I'd...I'd like to talk with you for a few moments, whenever it suits you, whenever you can.

GLORIA: Who are you?

GIRL: I'm a third-year student at the School of Dramatic Arts. I'm studying to be an actress. (GLORIA *looks her up and down, with an interest that's slightly more sincere.*)

GLORIA: Oh, so you want to be an actress. Are you any good?

Pause.

GIRL: Yes.

GLORIA: I'm glad to see you aren't modest. (*From this point on,* GLORIA *expresses herself tersely but with a certain seductive warmth.*)

GIRL: I'll try to explain to you why I'm here. They're planning to do a play about the actress Empar Ribera. About her early years. The director came to the School of Dramatic Arts to look for new faces. If possible, they intend to choose an unknown. You . . . know what Ribera was like.

GLORIA: I didn't know her at the beginning of her career. But I lived through the end of it.

GIRL: I really shouldn't dare ask you . . . for an interview. I know it's not possible. But if I could have just a few minutes. Anytime would be great for me.

GLORIA: What do you want to know?

GIRL: Things about her. You could tell me. The truth is . . . the director has already chosen four possible contenders for the part, one of them is me, and he wants us to audition. One of the four will get the part. I would like to know what Empar Ribera was like . . . so that I'd understand her better.

GLORIA: How many contenders? Four?

GIRL: Yes.

GLORIA: Four. (SHE *smiles enigmatically.*) And only one of you will get the part. Have you acted professionally before?

GIRL: No.

GLORIA: It would be the first time.

GIRL: Yes.

GLORIA: You must be joking.

GIRL: It's no joke to me, not in the slightest. I want to prepare myself to read for the part. If you would agree to talk to me a while about Ribera, I know it sounds silly, but maybe it would help me create the character.

GLORIA: Indeed it would. You can be sure of that.

GIRL: I'm sorry to bother you with this, Miss Marc.

GLORIA: It won't be easy. They've crucified me with appointments that half the time amount to nothing. Stupidities. But I'll look in my engagement book to see if I can fit you in somewhere. (SHE *takes her engagement book from a bag and turns some pages as* SHE *goes on talking.*) You haven't told me what you think about my show. An aspiring actress; the kind of audience that scares me most.

GIRL: I loved it! The way you have of moving from one register to another! . . . How did it ever occur to you to perform, alone, all those monologues and fragments of women characters of the great playwrights?

GLORIA: (*Looks up a moment.*) I'm not exactly young, you see. There are a lot of plays I'd dreamed of performing someday, but will never have the chance. So this has been my way of reclaiming some of them before any more time passes . . . before it's too late. (SHE *looks at her engagement book an instant, puts it away and then starts walking, followed by the* GIRL.) Let's see if the time suits you. Would it matter if we saw each other at my house?

GIRL: On the contrary. I was certain you were going to say no. Thank you so much, Miss Marc!

GLORIA: (*Beginning her exit.*) We share the same profession: call me Gloria. Empar Ribera was the best. There was no one to compare with her. No one. And if you hear them say I'm her successor, don't believe it. I'm not. Ribera was Ribera. I am I. That's it.

Exits. With her the side curtain that had marked this scene also disappears, and in its place is a television camera or some electronic device of the kind that can be found in television studios. The GIRL *has remained onstage. Another mature woman, with strong features, dressed in a sporty, comfortable outfit, enters. SHE is speaking alone, perhaps to someone offstage, but not necessarily.*

ANGELA: If you don't know how to do television, then go wait tables. An incompetent director, an incompetent producer, and actors who're even more incompetent! Where did they find them anyhow? Probably under a rock somewhere. But not to worry, we have stupid Angela Roca on the set. She'll pick up the pieces and solve all your problems! Well, my friends, they pay me to show the silly face that God gave me on the screen and make the public laugh at the clever things I say—not to wipe the noses and clean the asses of technicians who don't know where to place a camera and are scared shitless when I show my temper.

GIRL: Miss Roca.

ANGELA: (*Abruptly.*) What is it?

GIRL: Could . . . could you spare me a second?

ANGELA: Did that nitwit in makeup send you?

GIRL: I . . .

ANGELA: Tell her for me that she's not going to touch my face again, not even if she's the last paint dauber left on earth! Next time, if there is a next time, I'll bring my own makeup artist. And tell production not to worry. I'll pay for it myself. Believe it or not, if a real professional does me, I come out looking sexier than those little farts that show off their tits and end up big successes—for about three weeks. But they can't read their lines because God didn't give them the ounce of intelligence necessary to speak like a human being.

GIRL: I'm not from makeup.

ANGELA: Well, where the hell did you come from? Are you an extra in the show? Do you want to be a success in television, darling? Fine. It pays well. And if you manage to walk on once a week and belch, you'll be a success. Relax. Just do that and you'll be pop-u-lar. I'm pop-u-lar, too, and they pay me a small fortune to play the fool and make everyone say: Angela Roca, she's so adorable, and she talks just like an aunt of ours who's got a screw loose. Dear, they only do crap on television, but if you want to be a hit, then work in television. I spent twenty-five years as a stage actress, stirring up the dust in a lot of theatres, and I made a name for myself in the profession, in some decent plays—the kind that deal with the misery and the absurdities of life. But I couldn't say that I was a star. No way! What made me a star and rich was television. So, thank you, television. Do you get what I'm telling you? I've had it up to my ovaries! They won't see my face around here again! (*Shouting toward offstage.*) I'm going back to the stage! Well, I won't leave completely; there's a company that wants me to do a commercial for their perfected tampons which are guaranteed to minimize the monthly curse. With what they'll pay me for that one commercial I can live quite a while without a care in the world. Without a care, doing theatre. Yes, damn it, doing theatre!

GIRL: Are you really returning to the stage? That's what so many people were hoping.

ANGELA: What people? Who was hoping? I'll return to the stage, but not because anyone was hoping I would. Cut the bullshit! And since you work in television, what interest do you have in sending me back to the theatre? Are you one of those who're out to take my place?

GIRL: No!

ANGELA: But you will be successful. I don't doubt it! Even a hippopotamus can be successful in television.

GIRL: I don't work in television. I would like an interview with you.

ANGELA: (*With a start.*) What? Beat it, dear. It's time to go! I don't give interviews. I don't care to see my face in women's magazines! I don't let anyone photograph my home, I don't give exclusives to tell how my boyfriend walked out on me, and I don't let anyone surprise me when I walk out of the clinic after a facetuck. Because all of that belongs to my private life! And that matters only to me. All you journalists can go shove it up your asses! Even if you enjoy it, I don't care.

GIRL: I'm not a journalist.

ANGELA: Fantastic! Then you don't have any reason to ask me for an interview. (SHE *starts to go past the girl.*)

GIRL: It's another kind of interview. I'm from the School of Dramatic Arts. I'm studying to be an actress.

ANGELA: (*Pause.* ANGELA *stops and, for the first time, looks at her with interest.*) Well, well! Do they still teach acting as poorly as they used to? I went to the School of Dramatic Arts myself, and got nothing out of it. I couldn't find any professor there who could teach me a thing. No, I'm lying. There was one.

GIRL: Could I ask you if it was Empar Ribera?

Pause.

ANGELA: I don't have time to waste on you.

Pause. The GIRL looks at her anxiously.

ANGELA: Do you want me to tell you that Ribera was the greatest? (*Pause.*) You look like a babe in the woods, dear. (*Pause.*) Well, maybe we could get together for a little while and I'd tell you some things about Empar Ribera you'd never imagine. Now I just want to get out of this hole, this pie factory, and relax with a cold beer. What the hell do you want to know? You're going to have to convince me, in any case.

GIRL: I'll try, Miss Roca. Knowing things about Empar Ribera can help me, I think.

ANGELA: Don't call me "miss." I'm Angela Roca. Or simply Angela. It's an ordinary name for an ordinary person. But it's mine. And I wouldn't change it for any other. Just don't give me titles. And, oh yes. I don't know what you're up to, but I don't think that prying into Ribera's life is going to help you one bit. You get my meaning, dear?

SHE *exits. The* GIRL *watches her leave while the television apparatus disappears and a lectern takes its place; perhaps there is also an intermittent beam of light such as movie projectors make. A third mature woman enters, dressed soberly.* SHE *crosses and picks up some papers that are on the lectern.*

MARIA: We've finished for today. We start tomorrow morning at eight. Be on time, please. They start mixing at three-thirty, and the film has to be ready day after tomorrow.

The beam of light goes out. The GIRL *goes over to* MARIA.

GIRL: Are you Maria Caminal?

MARIA: (*Calmly.*) Yes. Were you looking for me?

GIRL: I certainly was! And it wasn't easy to locate you.

MARIA: I don't do auditions for dubbers.

GIRL: No. I don't need work, not at the moment at least. And I don't have film dubbing in mind. That's not why I was looking for you.

MARIA: Go on.

GIRL: I've been told that you knew the actress Empar Ribera.

MARIA: Oh? That was quite a few years back.

GIRL: But you did know her, right?

MARIA: Yes. Is that why you came to see me?

GIRL: Exactly.

MARIA: Who told you about me?

GIRL: I did some investigating. You studied at the School of Dramatic Arts. Gloria Marc and Angela Roca were in the same class as you. The three of you were there at the same time.

MARIA: More or less.

GIRL: You were friends, I suppose.

MARIA: Yes, good friends.

GIRL: And afterwards, did you continue to be?

MARIA: We see one another from time to time. Yes, you could say that we're still friends. Well, so it would appear. In any event, Gloria and Angela are having dinner at my house on Monday.

GIRL: (*Fascinated.*) Ah! . . .

MARIA: (*To herself.*) Just the three of us. That hasn't happened in a long time. (*To the* GIRL.) It's not necessary for me to explain that to you.

GIRL: (*Persisting.*) After you graduated, your careers went in , different directions.

MARIA: Especially mine. After a while I left the theatre and ended up dubbing films.

GIRL: Did you lose interest in the theatre?

MARIA: (*Bluntly.*) What do you want?

GIRL: I'm in my third year at the School of Dramatic Arts.

MARIA: You, too.

GIRL: And I'm looking for someone to help me.

MARIA: It's hard to be really good.

GIRL: I know.

MARIA: It's a tough profession.

GIRL: That doesn't matter to me.

MARIA: It will. How did you know you wanted to be an actress?

GIRL: My parents gave me a toy theatre. I used to play with it for hours.

MARIA: Oh, yes. Toy theatres. They're beautiful. Especially the old ones they used to make. I had one once upon a time. It didn't last long.

GIRL: I still have mine. I played with it continually when I was a child. I would even put on a costume and imagine that I could step on the little stage and act with the cardboard figures. (*Change of tone.*) Will you help me?

MARIA: What can I say? If necessary . . .

GIRL: I need someone to explain to me what Empar Ribera was like.

MARIA: Oh, no. I couldn't be of any help with that.

GIRL: Why not?

MARIA: I don't know what she was like. I did know her but I never knew what she was really like, inside.

GIRL: I'm going to have . . . to have an audition. For a role with a professional company. My first part. And it's the lead. They won't give it to me—I have no illusions about that—but I still have to give it a try.

MARIA: Oh, you have plenty of illusions. I know all about that. What kind of a play is it?

GIRL: It's about the life of Empar Ribera. (MARIA *bursts out laughing.*) It's a beautiful play.

MARIA: I'm sure it is. Forgive me. (*Jokingly.*) About all her life?

GIRL: Only the early years.

MARIA: Oh, then it will have a happy ending.

GIRL: Will you help me? You could tell me your memories of her.

MARIA: Yes. Why not? We'll find us an evening. I never really understood her at all, but so be it, I'll tell you about those times.

GIRL: Does all this sound crazy to you?

MARIA: Why?

GIRL: I don't know if learning about her will really help me perform on a stage.

MARIA: Maybe it will, maybe it won't. You'll have to decide that for yourself.

GIRL: When can we get together?

MARIA: Almost any day. Except Monday. I have that dinner, remember? That's a standing obligation. By the way, why don't you call me Maria?

LIGHTS DOWN

SCENE TWO

Lights up. GLORIA, ANGELA, *and* MARIA *seated at a table which exhibits the remains of a dinner. Behind them we see the bare walls of the stage.*

GLORIA: It's only in the planning stages. And it has to be kept secret. We don't want anyone to find out.

MARIA: Don't look at me. You're the ones who'll let it slip out.

ANGELA: But in principle, what do you think?

MARIA: I don't think anyone's been holding their breath to see you together on the stage. But if it works out, it could be sensational. And, of course, I'll have a chance to direct again.

GLORIA: The dates are perfect for me, the production company is about as solvent as you can find these days, and the creative team's the very best. And with Maria directing, the rehearsals are certain to be harmonious.

ANGELA: Well, I'm curious to know who's doing the part of Borkman.

GLORIA: The part hasn't been cast yet, but that won't be a problem.

ANGELA: But I'd like to know. It's all the same to me whether I play Gunhilda or Ella. You decide that, Gloria. But the actor who does Borkman has to be up to it. (*A glance at* MARIA, *who has closed her eyes.*) Let's change the subject; Maria's going to sleep on us.

MARIA: (*Reacting strongly.*) It interests me very much, silly. Go on, I'm listening. It's just that suddenly I wasn't feeling so well.

GLORIA: Do you have a headache?

MARIA: Something like that.

ANGELA: Take a pain killer. I have something in my purse, if you want one.

MARIA: It'll pass soon.

ANGELA: I should see a doctor myself. After all these months of taping the show, I feel like I've been hit by a truck. He can't cure me, but he can give me some relief. When Francisco died, that invisible monster who's always waiting to pounce, gave me one hell of a bite. And he left his teeth in me, so I'd never forget. As if I ever could.

GLORIA: How long has it been? Three years?

ANGELA: Yes, three goddamn years.

GLORIA: I wanted to go to the funeral, but I was in Belgium, and it . . .

ANGELA: . . . was too far.

GLORIA: I would have come, even if I'd been in China. The problem was the dress rehearsal for the opera I was directing in Brussels; I simply couldn't leave.

ANGELA: It was worse than when my mother died. With Francisco I always felt protected, even though he was only three years older than me . . . How can I tell you? That awful night, a telephone call, running to the hospital . . . an accident . . . His left eye half protruding from the socket . . . But he could see me with the other one. I held his hand . . . He knew that he was dying. And I pretended it wasn't so. After all, I'm an actress. But the monster was already there between us. It was too much.

MARIA: Can you just shut up for a minute about your monster?

ANGELA: It's obvious that my monster has never paid you a visit.

MARIA: I must not be important enough.

ANGELA: I guess you've just put me in my place.

MARIA: I'm allowed to.

ANGELA: How's your headache?

MARIA: Better. I'm managing.

GLORIA: (*To* ANGELA.) When your lover died, you still had your husband . . . and friends. When Sean passed away, I had no one to turn to.

ANGELA: What good was my husband? And friends are no help.

MARIA: Well, thanks.

ANGELA: You know what I mean. And my husband can go to hell.

GLORIA: Well, I could have used a friend for those three weeks. It's been almost a year. You don't know what it was like. They told me that his illness was terminal, that he couldn't live more than two weeks. I took the first plane and landed in London. He was hooked up to tubes. At least he was in the hospital and not at home. But his wife spent hours at his bedside, and I was only his lover. I tried to speak with her, to reach an agreement, but she refused to see me.

MARIA: Naturally.

GLORIA: I was the one Sean loved! When I finally managed to get into his room, I lay down beside him on the bed, I unbuttoned my dress so that he could touch me, and . . . I felt his penis under the sheet. A nurse threw a fit, and Sean—he still had his sense of humor—invited her to join the party . . . But for three long weeks—not the two weeks they'd said—I saw him only three or four times. I spent the rest of the time in my hotel room, watching television and waiting for the phone to ring. Alone. Always alone. If only you could have been there with me, Maria.

MARIA: I would have only told you scary stories. Lately, I've become an expert in scary stories.

GLORIA: At least I would have had you with me. All I could do was count the minutes and the seconds.

ANGELA: More and more people we love are dying.

MARIA: Don't overdramatize it. When Anna died, neither of you made a big fuss. (*Pause.* SHE *smiles maliciously and looks at them askance.*) Of course, we were all much younger then.

Pause.

ANGELA: Why did you bring up Anna? A lot of water has passed under the bridge since then. You're acting strange.

GLORIA: I agree.

MARIA: Well, I'll change the subject. I invited you here to dinner so that we'd have a chance to talk about the Ibsen production, which I truly hope you'll agree to. Just to see you two confront each other onstage . . .

GLORIA: I don't like the way you put that. We wouldn't be confronting each other.

MARIA: Anyhow, it would be the fulfillment of a dream to see the two of you together, for the first time, on a stage. My two favorite witches together.

ANGELA: Is an expression of gratitude required?

MARIA: Well, there are still some details to be worked out. And first Gloria and I need to talk a few minutes about the dubbing of her film.

GLORIA: (*With sudden enthusiasm.*) Yes! (*To* ANGELA.) You've heard, haven't you, that Maria is going to direct the dubbing of the film I made in Italy?

ANGELA: Who hasn't heard!

GLORIA: It's going to be great! The film's stupid, of course. But just knowing that I'll be working with Maria . . . I got so excited when they told me.

MARIA: It means that much to you?

GLORIA: I'll feel safe in your hands.

MARIA: We'll have it finished in a couple of days.

GLORIA: The two of us together again, after so many years.

MARIA: It's only a dubbing studio, not a theatre. The only thing that counts is your voice.

GLORIA: I'm devastated. For you it's just another dubbing job.

MARIA: I love you. No, it won't be just another dubbing job. Not for me. It will be two special days. I've scheduled your takes in four sessions. You won't have to get up early or tire yourself out too much. We start at eleven in the morning and return at four in the afternoon. If you're not happy with any take, you can repeat it until you're satisfied. How does that sound?

GLORIA: Perfect! I love you.

MARIA: Then it's all settled. Now you can get back to more important matters. I'll listen to everything you say. I may close my eyes from time to time but I'll be listening.

ANGELA: (*To* MARIA.) Darling, you really do have balls! (SHE *laughs with amusement.*)

GLORIA: What's so funny?

ANGELA: Me. Doesn't everyone say I'm a laugh riot? But poor Maria is utterly bored with me.

MARIA: That's not true.

ANGELA: I can't help it. I've seen audiences sobbing over one of my dramatic portrayals. But they prefer me as a comic actress. It would be all the same whether I rant about the evil that's overtaking the world or simply fart. The minute I open my mouth they start laughing. Nobody takes me seriously.

GLORIA: (*Ironically.*) Oh, reallly?

ANGELA: It's the same everywhere. I get home worn out from work, in a foul mood from the events of the day, and fed up with the whole fucking world.

GLORIA: I can imagine.

ANGELA: I find the man I live with stretched out in his recliner. Even though there's no difference between talking to him and talking to a piece of furniture, he at least looks like a person. So I make him the butt of all my complaints, letting out my anger on him, getting it out of my system, talking nonstop until I don't make any sense at all. He just looks at me and smiles, with that silly smile of complicity he always has, never losing his calm in the slightest. He infuriates me so much that once, just to annoy him, I . . . It just slipped out, I couldn't stop in time. I'd damned to hell everybody and everything, with no reaction from him. So, whammy, apropos of nothing I'd been saying, I told him I'd had a lover. Me, not him. He was silent for a moment. Then he opened his mouth, and do you know what he said? "It's impossible to get bored around you. You always make me laugh." I had admitted for the first and only time in my life the existence of my lover. And all he could say was I made him laugh. (*Shift.*) And so, I have to confess, I must be funny.

MARIA: If you'd ever shut up long enough, I'd tell you what I think about you.

ANGELA: I know you don't love me. You only love Gloria.

MARIA: I've told her I love her. And I always demonstrated it to you when the need arose.

GLORIA: (*Long Pause.*) Sean died, and even though he was the man I loved most, there's another man in my life now. Life does go on. I don't intend to die mourning the past. I've made love with a pianist who excited me and turned me on playing Mozart. I had a brief and shameful affair with one of those brutes who are into sports; he would crush me in his arms and weep over his luck in being able to screw a lady like me. For a while, whenever I went out I had bodyguards who made me disguise myself in the most unusual ways, only because my boyfriend was a government minister. And afterwards . . . or maybe it was before, there was a boy of seventeen—Italian, like a painting of the Venetian school, who never got enough and became a sweet and loving pupil. And since it's just the three of us here, I'm going to confess: I met a beautiful lesbian and I asked myself, why not? With sex or without it, I've had some connection with half the interesting people who've appeared in the culture section of the Sunday papers. And all of it thanks to the theatre. Most of all the stage has given me nights of phosphorescent intensity, nights of total emotional intoxication. So many, I wouldn't know which to choose. Or maybe I do. When I did Clytemnestra in the Roman theatre of Herod Anticus beneath the Acropolis. My voice spoke words near the stones where those same words, by history's first dramatists, were spoken for the first time in another language. I remember I raised my face to the sky to contemplate the vault of stars as I spoke my lines, and I felt that the centuries were mingling, that time was disappearing. For an instant I had conquered the monster. (*Pause. SHE changes. Now lighter.*) I still haven't performed at Epidaurus. But one can't ask for everything. In my own way I've had control of my life, don't you think? (*Pause.*) I have to pee. I'll be right back. (*Exits.*)

Pause.

MARIA: Our girl has been around.

ANGELA: And had a few fucks along the way. (*Pause. ANGELA gets up. SHE will imitate GLORIA seriously, almost without parody, while from time to time SHE will add her own commentary.*) "In my own way I've had control of my life. I played Clytemnestra." . . . I don't like those Clytemnestra types; I'm sorry, but Greek tragedy leaves me cold . . . "I did Clytemnestra in the Roman theatre of Herod Atticus, in Athens, beneath the Parthenon. An unforgettable night, a magical night, of phosphorescent intensity." What does phosphorescent intensity mean?

MARIA: Absolutely nothing.

ANGELA: "Phosphorescent. A night of emotional intoxication. I inflated like a balloon and ascended to heaven. Only one regret gnaws at me: I still haven't acted at the Vatican, in St. Peter's square, before the Pope." (GLORIA *has entered behind* ANGELA, *who, acting facing* MARIA, *doesn't see her. And* MARIA *hasn't let on that* GLORIA *is there.*) "Am I a frustrated woman? Not as much as you two, perhaps, because I've made love with a Venetian painting . . . , and with an orangutan from the African jungle . . . and with a lesbian. Or maybe it was two lesbians. In that respect I've succeeded in equaling you know who. In that respect I have equaled that awful beast who played with our future lives. I've reached the pinnacle. And now I have to piss. I'll be right back." (SHE *turns round to go and finds herself face to face with* GLORIA. *An instant of surprise. Then* SHE *observes a smiling* GLORIA *and quickly reacts.*) Maria, you are an evil bitch. (SHE *bows to* GLORIA.) The curtain falls. (GLORIA *applauds.*)

GLORIA: Bravo, bravo, bravo! (*To* MARIA.) Thanks for not interrupting the show.

MARIA: So I'm an evil bitch. Well, that makes me not so different from the two of you.

GLORIA: Sit down, Angela. Now it's my turn.

The two women look at each other.

ANGELA: Am I really to have this honor?

GLORIA: I could do no less.

ANGELA: Then I'll be sitting on the edge of my seat. (SHE *sits down.* GLORIA *begins to mimic* ANGELA *with resentment that grows and prevents an authentic imitation.*)

GLORIA: "I hate television. Television has made me pop-u-lar. I'm not interested in being pop-u-lar. Any little tart with an ass and silicon breasts can be pop-u-lar. I'm an actress. But, of course, I like money, so I've made a few sacrifices. Now I have a million or two and I can shit on the job that made me rich. However, along the way, I became a national clown. Oh, what an injustice. I'm not really a clown." Why are you so unhappy about being a clown . . . ? "Please, I'm an actress. An actress who can play any role. Drama or comedy. Tragedy or farce. No, not tragedy. Not with all those tunics and the funny shoes . . . Ugh. How ridiculous. And not clowns either. They're puppets without a soul . . . No, I prefer the half-tones. A drama, a play, the in-betweens. And a calm life. Also half and half, to be sure. Of course, sometimes I feel a kind of nostalgia . . ." Nostalgia for what? Do you remember? How many years has it been since that end of spring and beginning of summer? Nostalgia for what, Angela? I'm not sure if it's nostalgia you feel. Maybe envy is the right word. (*Pause.* SHE *sits down.*)

ANGELA: You're a magnificent actress, but you should leave the imitations to me.

MARIA: Why don't we all have a drink?

ANGELA: You and I have made slightly different choices in life, Gloria dear.

GLORIA: That's for sure.

MARIA: If you don't want a drink, now that you've eaten, you can leave. I have a headache I can't get rid of.

ANGELA: Bring the drinks, take two aspirin, and listen to me. That one and I have a few more words to say to each other, and you are the ideal audience.

GLORIA: What more do you need to say when I can read your mind? Huh? What can you say to me that I don't already know?

ANGELA: At least I can get it out of my system.

GLORIA: But I haven't finished. So it's my turn first.

MARIA: With or without ice?

ANGELA: Ice.

GLORIA: Three cubes. Now let me finish. About your envy. I've felt it all evening. Aside from your man at home in his recliner, aside from that piece of furniture—I believe those were your words—who for certain is unfaithful to you with every secretary in his office . . .

ANGELA: Oh, what a discovery! You've just destroyed my life!

GLORIA: . . . aside from him, you've had only one other man make love to you in your whole fucking life.

MARIA: Don't be vulgar. Vulgarity is Angela's specialty.

GLORIA: One single lover! And it wouldn't surprise me if that one was all in your head.

ANGELA: So what?

GLORIA: Nothing. It was only an example. Drama and comedy. But never a step beyond. The absolute mediocrity of an individual who has never dared to live and who'll die terrified by all she let slip through her fingers. You have been satisfied to suffocate in provincial mediocrity, without the courage to step over a few mountains that are like cardboard boxes and cross a sea that's merely a puddle. You made the choices, my dear. Go ahead and envy me, if that makes you happy, but don't try to put your claws in me! Claw the one who's to blame for your problems. Claw your own face. That's not a bad idea. It might improve your looks. That last operation left your face a mess.

ANGELA: Your face, on the other hand, which is beginning to look hopelessly moth-eaten, has maintained for more years than anyone can remember a certain international seal of approval. The great Gloria Marc, from one plane to the next, from one festival to another, always surrounded by the beautiful people whose faces appear on the covers of glossy magazines. But you were always very careful not to slip, not to be out of step, serving up to a public of famous mummies the menu they'll accept. A five star lunch: pure sterilized and perfumed shit wrapped in tinfoil!

GLORIA: Vulgarly put. Perhaps at one time or another I have had to smile and accept a kiss with more revulsion than pleasure. But I swear that I've made my own way. Without fear, with guts, without regrets afterwards! During that spring and summer that you and I remember so well, I learned that people are alone. An important discovery! I kept going on, farther and farther, my art and I, as far as I could go. And I'm not complaining about what I've achieved.

ANGELA: Meanwhile, I stayed right here, working in my own little world, acting in plays that didn't talk about gods and heroes, or cosmic forces, or the great profundities. No, I was in plays about ordinary people of flesh and blood—my neighbors and their silly problems—as mediocre as I am. And finding my salvation in them, even if only for a moment;

saving ourselves together through theatre, but not through serving theatre. It was through serving them, the ones who come to see us act. Do you understand that? I haven't had a lot of lovers, that's true; but now I realize I've never been alone!

GLORIA: You're so naive! We're always alone!

MARIA: (*Pause.*) I suspect we aren't going to do that play together. (*Silence.*) It would have been worth the wait. What a shame!

GLORIA: It's late. I'm going home. Where did I put my purse?

MARIA: A few moments more. I still haven't spoken about myself and my splendid career. I'll be brief because I'm tired and because neither of you is going to interrupt me. (*Pause. The* OTHER TWO *exchange looks; perhaps they shrug their shoulders, and perhaps they sit in silence.*) Thanks. My stupendous career. Well, before the end of that spring Gloria was speaking about, I really intended to be an actress. All four of us did. We three . . . and Anna. However, when summer was over, I decided to try my hand at directing. It was something I knew I could do well—but the jobs were few and far between. So I became a film dubber to survive. And that's what I've remained. I give my voice to a real actress, changing her language into mine. I try to do it well. I'm a true professional. I also direct the voices that other actresses dub. I try to do that well, too. I know what you're thinking. A measly job, a job hardly worth mentioning. At least unworthy of your talents. An ephimeral job at best, or so it seems to me. A hundred years ago dubbing didn't exist. And in another hundred years it won't exist again. There'll be some other way, who knows what. And then someone will hear the word "dubbing" on some old soundtrack and they won't understand it. It will have lost its meaning. And what a pity! Don't you feel sorry for me? I do, I'm your mirror. You two can fight each other, you can argue which of you had more triumphal nights, but it will all pass, you and your memory, and also the memory of the great and not-so-great plays you've acted in. Why don't you just take it calmly? Let a bit more time pass and, I venture to say, even Shakespeare will disappear. Shakespeare? It's only a question of time. (*Pause.*) There is no future. Nothing is immortal. In your hearts you pretend otherwise. No, I'm sorry. Nothing. Knowing that helps me to go forward with a certain serenity and without bitterness. Without any resentment at all about old stories from the past. (*Pause.*) Well, maybe I do still have a bit of resentment. (*Pause.*) Speaking of other things, do you know what they say about you, Gloria? That you're frigid. And do you know what they say about you, Angela? That you've passed over the bodies of everyone who got in your way. (*Pause.*) Now you can go. Good night.

LIGHTS DOWN

SCENE THREE

Lights up. Elements of a chaotic interior. Some books. A telephone. In the background, the bare walls of the stage. GLORIA *receives the* GIRL *who enters with a bouquet of flowers.*

GLORIA: Come in. Come in and sit down.

GIRL: (*Offers her the flowers.*) Here. They're for you.

GLORIA: For me? But, why did you do that? They're lovely. You shouldn't have.

GIRL: I thought of it at the last moment. An impulse. So I bought them.

GLORIA: I'll leave them here. They'll brighten the room while we're talking. What would you like to drink?

GIRL: Nothing right now.

GLORIA: I don't have much variety to offer you. This apartment is a mess. I'm always on the go and I don't spend much time here. I should find someone I can trust to make the place presentable. Or maybe I'll leave it all and move to the country for good . . . We'll see. How did your audition go?

GIRL: It hasn't happened yet. And it turns out that there are two.

GLORIA: Two contenders or two auditions?

GIRL: Two auditions on different days. The contenders are still the same.

GLORIA: Four of you.

GIRL: You remember.

GLORIA: I know the director. I almost contracted him to direct me in a play once. He's not the greatest but at least he has some good ideas. And a lot of them don't.

GIRL: I've seen some productions of his that weren't bad.

GLORIA: Does he know that you've come to see me?

GIRL: No! I'd never tell him! I'd be too embarrassed.

GLORIA: Well, he happens to know.

GIRL: How?

GLORIA: I told him myself.

Pause.

GIRL: What?

GLORIA: He came to see my show and came backstage afterwards. He told me about his project, and I told him that one of the girls he'd chosen to audition for the lead had an appointment with me so that I could tell her something about the character.

Pause.

GIRL: And . . . how did he react?

GLORIA: You're not his favorite, but he asked me to observe you and give him my opinion afterwards.

Pause.

GIRL: I think I'd better leave.

GLORIA: Really? You overcame your timidity to ask me for an interview, and now that you have it, you want to leave?

GIRL: It's just . . . I'm sorry. It's just that . . .

GLORIA: The situation has changed.

GIRL: Yes.

GLORIA: It's changed for the better. Now there are other eyes looking at you. You said you were good.

GIRL: I didn't come here to audition for you, Miss Marc.

GLORIA: Leave off the Miss Marc. What an obsession! Call me Gloria. No one said you came here for any audition. I'm the one who's being auditioned. You came here to pick my brains. My memories of Empar Ribera. Don't you want to hear them?

Pause.

GIRL: Yes.

GLORIA: So forget about the auditions. They don't have to be the opportunity of a lifetime.

GIRL: You aren't making it easy for me to forget about them.

GLORIA: Stop worrying and ask me something. Whatever you wish.

GIRL: Right now I'd like a whisky, if possible.

GLORIA: I do have whisky. Ice?

GIRL: Three cubes.

GLORIA: To be sure. (*Shift.*) Empar Ribera. I wanted to be an actress and she gave me my first big push. Pushes can be dangerous. They can make you fall on your face. But her push got me off to a flying start.

GIRL: In the role of Iphigenia.

GLORIA: In the role of Iphigenia.

GIRL: It must have been a great night.

GLORIA: I only remember moments of it.

GIRL: And after that, did she keep on helping you?

GLORIA: She died shortly afterwards, in the town where she'd been born, in her brother's house. I took the train and went to her funeral. A huge crowd was there. All sorts of dignitaries and her brother Enric Ribera, an actor as important as she was—or even more.

GIRL: Did you see them act together?

GLORIA: A couple of times, I think. Before I entered the School of Dramatic Art.

GIRL: Did you like them?

GLORIA: I felt an obligation to be impressed. They were the most acclaimed actors of their time. Then, for a while, I doubted that I'd really liked them. And when I finally met her, I decided that, yes, they had impressed me.

GIRL: Did you meet her at the School of Dramatic Art?

GLORIA: Not immediately. You know, I'll have to talk about myself as much as Empar Ribera.

GIRL: That doesn't matter. It all interests me.

GLORIA: Do you really mean it, or are you just trying to be polite?

GIRL: (*Slow to react.*) What?

GLORIA: (*Smiles.*) You can't help it. You're trying to make me like you.

GIRL: (*Timidly.*) Why do you talk to me that way? (*Stands up.*) You don't really want me to forget about the auditions. Let's leave it at that.

GLORIA: Wait! Wait! Sit down! If we speak frankly we avoid misunderstandings. Take it as a joke. Laugh at yourself. And at me, too. (*The* GIRL *sits down.*) Will you? Try it at least.

GIRL: If I don't, you'll have a horrible opinion of me, for sure.

GLORIA: Now I do like you! (SHE *laughs.*) I entered the School of Dramatic Art full of illusions and I was utterly disappointed.

GIRL: The same thing happened to me.

GLORIA: But it doesn't matter. You have to stick with it anyhow.

GIRL: Yes. I learned that, too.

GLORIA: Very few dreams come true the way you imagined they would. In any case, the situation at the school was dreadful. Grimy classrooms, professors shedding dandruff, nothing but cobwebs and pomposity. Then, suddenly, in the second year, she appeared. Empar Ribera, a sacred monster, who was deigning to come down to share her wisdom with us.

GIRL: And then?

GLORIA: The most impatient students received her with total skepticism. It was when I was still doubting that I'd really liked her performances. What could she teach us? An old woman with haughty airs who walked in a ridiculous way with short, tiny steps. We were looking at a dinosaur who, with her brother, had received every official recognition imaginable, and the best thing she could do now was to die and leave the theatre to us.

GIRL: And the classes began.

GLORIA: Yes. And we discovered to our surprise that this wrinkled and painted old woman understood us as no one had before, and inspired us as no one had before. It was like discovering the theatre all over again.

GIRL: Really.

GLORIA: You should have seen her! Full of curiosity, asking us where we were from and what our ambitions were . . . They weren't the kind of classes we were used to. She would gather us around her like a mother hen, she'd joke with us and deliberately provoke us to get over our shyness. Or she would turn serious and tell us that the ethic of theatre is the ethic of life. (SHE *laughs without really knowing why.*) And so, all of a sudden, we found ourselves talking about theatre, about the Greeks and modern playwrights. She would laugh, for example, about the dreadful plays she sometimes found herself performing over her long career . . . Then, suddenly, without missing a beat, she would extend her arm in a gesture that seemed to sweep away all trivial talk, and breaking the silence she'd created, she would begin to perform one of her roles. A raspy voice, at least at that point, a voice that let every word fall like lead. She'd go on and on, and then, with a shriek, she'd stop and say no, no she shouldn't have spoken those lines. They needed a young voice. And then she'd seem to be searching among the students, point to one of us, put the book in our hands, push us to the front and ponder the situation: "It's over for me, it's finished, you're the one who must say those words about love . . ." And you'd feel at that moment that you were her successor, carrying on for Empar Ribera. And, yes, you'd begin to read strongly. But then she'd give you a hard time, grow impatient, let out a sigh and, finally, join you in speaking the lines in an outburst that was part joy and part victory, carrying the speech to its climax.

GIRL: No one ever taught me that way.

GLORIA: It wasn't an orthodox way of teaching. It was pure passion, nothing more. And we needed it.

GIRL: How did she manage to act in the theatre and not miss her classes?

GLORIA: You don't understand. Empar Ribera had retired. She didn't act anymore. She decided she'd had enough. Then they offered her the classes and she accepted. It was only for two years.

GIRL: Yes, I read about it.

GLORIA: Only our two years. No one had had her before and no one had her afterwards. We were the privileged ones, her only students. She had intended to teach only one year. She was feeling tired, but she came back the next year because we were a good class, she loved us or, at least, she liked us and didn't want to leave us stranded.

GIRL: Angela Roca was in that class, too.

GLORIA: And a lot of others. It was a good group. After a time, the relationship between her and us went beyond the walls of the school. She'd have us meet at her house; we'd talk for hours, she'd show us mementos, photographs, caricatures, newspaper clippings, objects she loved . . . One was an old toy theatre that had been built especially for her. A beautiful plaything. Have you ever seen one of those little theatres?

GIRL: I have one.

GLORIA: It couldn't be like hers. There wasn't a detail missing. It seemed real. Purple, blue, and gold, it was a delight.

GIRL: Purple, blue, and gold?

GLORIA: I could tell you about so many beautiful and curious things in her house . . . We used to look at them, touch them, ask her about them . . . Suddenly, she would have enough of that and have us or read lines. Then, at some point, she'd rise from the armchair where she always sat; a glance, an imperceptible gesture . . . and an invisible circle, a magic circle, would form around her. Her moment had come. She'd begin to recite, to act . . . in her own style, old-fashioned yet wonderful. Wrinkles, raspy voice and all, she was still quite marvelous. And just for us. Afterwards, if we were lucky, on a special day, she'd ask us, with a smile of complicity, if we'd please stay for dinner. The servant would protest but she'd laugh it off. We'd insist that we didn't want to be a bother, but Empar Ribera would chide the servant and joke about being an old woman who needed company now that her brother was far away. Having no choice, we'd agree and we'd stay with her until the wee hours of the morning. (*Pause.*) I consider it a privilege to have experienced those days . . . the golden age. (*Pause.*) Finally, when we were finishing our third year, the second with her, one night, toward the end of spring, after dinner at her house, she told us she was leaving the theatre for good, that her acting days were over. It was farewell. Except—and she used these very words—except that she had one last sign of her affection to bestow. She would direct *Iphigenia in Aulis*, one of the first plays she had acted in as a young girl, and the lead would go to one of the four of us.

GIRL: Four? There were only four of you in the class?

GLORIA: No, there were other girls and boys, too.

GIRL: Then why only four?

GLORIA: (*Pause.*)I'll explain. We four were the ones who really stood out in the class; four aspiring actresses. We were the ones, according to Ribera, who really gave tone to the class. I can't be modest about it. It was for the four of us that she continued giving classes the second year, in spite of her failing health. We had found her but she had also found us.

GIRL: What about the visits to her house, the dinners, the times you stayed until morning . . . ?

GLORIA: With only a few exceptions, they were reserved for the four of us—Anna, Angela, Maria, and myself. What did you think? That all the students in the class had dinner at Empar Ribera's home?

GIRL: Angela . . . was she Angela Roca?

GLORIA: Yes.

GIRL: And Maria. Could she be Maria Caminal?

GLORIA: How do you know her name?

GIRL: I think she works in film, as a dubber . . .

GLORIA: You are well informed. A delightful girl.

GIRL: The fourth, Anna. I don't know who she is.

GLORIA: Anna died. I'm indebted to her. Empar Ribera had trained us. She had instilled in us an ethic of the theatre, a way of understanding the theatre, not as a religion but as a way of thinking and living. To demonstrate it she wanted to direct *Iphigenia*. She had been offered an open-air theatre, and that summer one of us would be Iphigenia.

GIRL: It was you.

GLORIA: No, wait. Ribera wasn't sure yet. She wanted a special Iphigenia, her Iphigenia. You know the plot: the king wants to go off to war, a just war, and the winds fail to come to fill the sails of his ships. Finally, the gods speak. A sacrifice is required to move the fleet, the sacrifice of the king's daughter, Iphigenia. She is to be sacrificed for the common good. After the immolation, the sails will fill and the ships will reach Troy. The common good takes precedence over the welfare of one person. Iphigenia would have to walk calmly to her death. Which of us would express that acceptance with most artistry? I suppose it wasn't easy for her to decide. She chose Anna.

GIRL: But you played the part.

GLORIA: That was afterwards. Two weeks being the opening, Anna got sick. She had to give up the part. Ribera had been directing energetically, it was her last effort, and among theatre people—among people who really love theatre—there was a growing sense of expectation. But now there was no Iphigenia. And as I said, it was only two weeks until the opening. It was then, only then, that I got the part. "Do you dare?" Empar Ribera asked me. She was asking but her face wasn't offering much encouragement. She looked exasperated but determined. I said yes. For two weeks I hardly slept. I studied, I rehearsed, I studied, I rehearsed. Iphigenia isn't the longest role in the play, but it's central to everything. I had to express the feelings of a virgin who, when she is about to marry the man she loves, accepts being sacrificed for the destiny of her people. Opening night the theatre was sold out. Ribera was helping me adjust my tunic, watching me, and then, at the last moment, she asked me again: Do you dare? I nodded yes and went on stage. (SHE *moves abruptly and starts searching among the books* SHE *has in the room.*) Where is it? It must be one of these. (SHE *takes a very worn book and thumbs through the pages.*) Here. Look. I'd almost forgotten. (SHE *reads.*) "Mother, I have given it much thought, so listen to me now" . . . That's almost the end of the play. "Mother, I have given it much thought, so listen to me now" . . . My voice isn't Iphigenia's voice anymore! You try it. Read the line.

GIRL: (*Surprised and frightened.*) Me? I couldn't.

GLORIA: Yes, you can. Try it. It'll be easy.

GIRL: No, I . . . just can't.

GLORIA: You could never say no in the presence of Empar Ribera. Do you want to know what she was like? Well, for one thing, it was dangerous to say no to her. Now read. Imagine that night. I'll explain it to you. Go ahead, read. "Mother, I've given it much thought, so listen to me now."

GIRL: (*Grabbing the book and reading intuitively.*) "Mother, I have given it much thought, so listen to me now."

GLORIA: Louder!

GIRL: "They have decided that I'm to die, and I want to die. Nobly, with no taint of cowardice."

GLORIA: "Nobly, with no taint of cowardice!" I felt Empar Ribera's presence, listening to every word, embracing me, urging me on with her eyes . . . Go on, don't stop.

GIRL: "You must understand, mother. All Greece, so powerful, has its eyes on me."

(*The* GIRL *tries to do it well, tries to concentrate.* GLORIA *directs her. Accompanying her words with gestures,* SHE *invites her to move and to imitate her.*)

GIRL: "Only through me can the ships set sail, to conquer the Trojans, to make sure the barbarians never return to lay waste our beloved land or rape the women of Greece."

GLORIA: And then I may have lifted my head. I don't remember; maybe I saw the audience for the first time in my life, or maybe I could only make out their shadows, maybe I sensed that they were the enemy I needed to conquer!

GIRL: "All this is what I gain by dying, this is my recompense for having returned freedom to Greece. And I will be happy."

GLORIA: "And I will be happy."

GIRL: "It would be wrong for you to hold my life too dearly now. I'm not yours, mother. I belong to Greece."

GLORIA: A certain arrogance! Say that line arrogantly! I was innocent but now I was also arrogant! And I had to conquer my enemy, the shadows out there in front of me! And another shadow sustained me, Empar Ribera, watching over me from offstage, protecting me.

GIRL: "All these men, an army of them, will venture forth to fight and die for their country. Do you want my life, this tiny life, to stand in their way? What answer would I have for them? What answer could I give if they asked me? What would you answer then if they asked you?"

GLORIA: Courage, courage! I didn't want to hear a single cough. Those sons of bitches who had paid to see me suffer were watching me without an ounce of pity, wanting to see if I was worth the price of admission. But now every last one of them had to keep quiet and submit to my words.

GIRL: "If a god wants my body, do you suppose I could oppose his divine will? No!"

GLORIA: No, no, no!

GIRL: "I offer my blood to the Greeks! Sacrifice me and march on to Troy! In death I'll find my marriage, my children, my victory! Let Greece smite the barbarians and let it remember its debt to me, that only because of me shall it be free! That only through me shall the barbarians be slaves!"

The GIRL *has read the lines as well as* SHE *could—furious, scared, and galvanized.*

Now SHE *stops and looks at* GLORIA.

GIRL: That's all of it.

GLORIA: No, it isn't! There are still a few more speeches. And the end came with that outburst: "Goodbye, light that I loved so much!" I left the stage and Ribera took me in her arms and said only one word: "Good!" And then the pigs who were seated out there began to applaud.

GIRL: Was I all right?

GLORIA: And instinct, hunger, rage, forced me back on stage to see if I really had won. But if you want to know what Empar Ribera was like, I'll tell you: she held me back, she grabbed my arm and held me back. She told me: "Let them wait. You must learn to be a greater bitch than they are.

GIRL: Miss Marc, how did I do?

GLORIA: In a few seconds she released me. "Now go." And I went back on stage. The applause grew louder. And I thought, now I've got you!

GIRL: Was I good?

GLORIA: And I took the first bow of my life. And then I knew I was an actress. That was only the beginning, and the game has never ended. Empar Ribera died, and I went to her funeral. I left some roses that mingled with the thousands of flowers that surrounded her, and I thought: "Thank you and goodbye, Empar Ribera." I've never left the stage since then. Until this day. Occasionally some idiot still writes that I'm the continuation of Empar Ribera. No way. Empar Ribera was great. And I'm only Gloria Marc.

GIRL: Tell me, how was I?

LIGHTS DOWN

SCENE FOUR

Lights up. Elements of a warm interior. Books, a telephone. Upstage, the bare walls. ANGELA *receives the* GIRL, *who enters with a pretty bouquet of flowers.*

ANGELA: Come in. Come in and sit down.

GIRL: (*Offering the flowers.*) Here, for you.

ANGELA: What's this, flowers for me? Did you think I was the Queen of England?

GIRL: I thought of it at the last moment. An impulse. So I bought them.

ANGELA: I'll find a pretty vase to put them in. They don't have much scent. Nowadays they're usually plastic.

GIRL: These are real!

ANGELA: I know that, dear. They're lovely. What would you like to drink?

GIRL: Nothing for the moment.

ANGELA: Well, I've got everything, and plenty of it. And if I don't, we'll send out for it.

GIRL: You have a lovely home.

ANGELA: It will be someday. It takes time, but bit by bit. I'll have it the way I want it by the time I'm seventy. Have you auditioned yet for that role?

GIRL: Once. But there's a callback. I don't feel too confident about it. It's very difficult, knowing they're comparing you with the others . . . Maybe, if they allowed me more time. .

ANGELA: (*Interrupting her.*) It'll turn out fine for you. If not this time, then the next. Well, aren't you going to ask me what I know about Empar Ribera? I warn you my memory's not so good. Besides, there are details about a person's life that are of no interest to anyone. But, go ahead, fire away.

GIRL: You knew Empar Ribera.

ANGELA: (*Interrupting her again.*) I'm going to have a whisky. Do you want one?

GIRL: Maybe. Yes.

ANGELA: A whisky for you . . .

GIRL: Wait, not so much.

ANGELA: I'm the one who shouldn't be drinking so much. Three cubes. How about you?

GIRL: Three for me, too.

ANGELA: Just look at her. She's imitating me.

GIRL: I always have three.

ANGELA: But, of course you do! Where were we?

GIRL: You knew Empar Ribera . . .

ANGELA: For a short time.

GIRL: I understand that she was your acting teacher at the School of Dramatic Art, Miss . . .

ANGELA: Don't be so formal. This is better between friends. Call me Angela.

GIRL: All right. Thanks.

ANGELA: Yes. She was my teacher for two years.

GIRL: What kind of relationship did she have with her students . . . with you?

ANGELA: Ribera had a way with words. Theatre was a sublime art; we must dedicate our lives to its cause . . . fantastic! From her lips it was this wonderful, heavenly music. But, you'll discover, reality is in the street and not in classrooms. I had lost my parents, but my older brother, God rest his soul, helped me financially as much as he could. The poor guy worked like a slave and he had to do without a lot of things to get ahead and try to give me a future. He paid my tuition for the third year, depriving himself of so much. No one ever loved me the way he did. But I was no slouch myself. When I finished my studies, which I could just as well have spared myself, I began to grab any small role they'd give me in the professional companies. Any role at all! I shut my eyes tight, I forgot about the Antigones and the Juliets, and did anything that would get me on stage to say three words and pay me a salary at the end of the week. I was cured of all inhibitions the day they gave me a contract to appear in a tacky burlesque show. They dyed my hair flaming red, dressed me in a bikini, and I had to show my skinny body to the audience and say a few stupidities to the leading man. But I was a young piece of flesh and that was what mattered.

GIRL: But what do you remember about Empar Ribera? . . .

ANGELA: We'll get around to Ribera. First I want to talk about your future. Until you manage to get a role that's halfway decent, you have to put up with a lot of crap. And maybe worse. The theatre is a very hard profession. And very wonderful, too. If it weren't, I'd work at something else. Look, keeping in mind that later I've had a great success in television, I could have said "To hell with your stupid plays" and worked only in TV. But no. No, indeed. There's nothing like the stage. Film isn't so bad . . . but it's not the same. The theatre has given me a lot of satisfaction, and a few bad experiences, too. Thanks to the theatre I've been able to play women like the ones you see in the street, real women who've been fucked by life, by men, and by the system . . . That's worth doing! You can play Clytemnestra any way you please. Lifting an eyebrow, wearing a divine costume, and screaming to heaven. You can do it the way you please because nobody has ever seen that lady. Who the fuck knows Clytemnestra? . . . But you see normal, ordinary women every day. Dare to play one of them! Do you want another drink?

GIRL: No.

ANGELA: I do. I need it to get myself started. That's how I am. Don't worry, we'll talk about la Ribera now. What do you want to know about her?

GIRL: They say . . . they say she had a great influence on you . . .

ANGELA: Who says so?

GIRL: I don't know. I read it somewhere . . .

ANGELA: For a start: Empar Ribera was a lesbian.

GIRL: What?

ANGELA: No big deal. I have the greatest respect for lesbians. Sometimes they can be better company than a man, or don't you think so?

GIRL: (*Who can't believe what* SHE *has heard.*) She was a lesbian? Are you sure?

ANGELA: Ribera? Christ! The only man she ever got in bed with was her brother!

GIRL: What? What do you mean? With her brother . . . ? What brother?

ANGELA: What brother do you think? Hers! She only had one! The great actor Enric Ribera. They made a magnificent pair! On stage together they were perfectly attuned. And in bed, too, obviously.

GIRL: It leaves me a little . . .

ANGELA: Wake up, dear! Why everyone knows it. There's even a play, inspired by them, that speaks of the tender love between a brother and sister who were actors. That's not the one you want to do, is it?

GIRL: No, hardly. The play I'm trying out for takes place during Empar Ribera's youth, when she . . .

ANGELA: (*Interrupting her.*) Yes, fine. Look, Ribera was a good teacher. We students drooled over her. She loved us very much. She was in her element with us. Wrinkled as a raisin, with her face ridiculously painted, but still, at her age, a unique actress. She's had imitators, or successors, or whatever you want to call them . . . but nothing really like her. I don't mean that there haven't been great actresses since her, take me for instance, but we're different. She was a great teacher, a great actress, a great lesbian. But you had to be careful not to fall into her clutches. You can only understand her enthusiasms and manipulations when you consider that she was drawn to women like a child to candy. And at Drama School, in my class, we were a group of very promising young things. She made us her own.

GIRL: What do you mean?

ANGELA: No, not what you're thinking. She would take us to her home. A house full of photographs and objects and memories . . .

GIRL: She had a beautiful toy theatre, didn't she?

ANGELA: (*Looks at her carefully.*) Who told you that?

GIRL: I read it somewhere. It caught my attention. I love those toy theatres myself.

ANGELA: That one was special. I've never seen another one just like it. And the crimson curtain—or maybe it was purple—had a design, and on the lower edge a pair of initials: E and R.

GIRL: (*Excited.*) Of course! The initials of Empar Ribera!

ANGELA: (*Pointedly.*) They weren't only hers. They were her brother's, too. Enric Ribera. Brother and sister, two names and the same initials. Two people joined as one. You get it, don't you? Enric Ribera had that theatre built to remember always, discreetly, the love he had for his sister. Two initials on the symbol of the art that united them: a cardboard theatre. (*Pause.*) Very romantic. What's wrong, dear? You look distracted. Are you listening to me?

GIRL: I'm sorry. Yes.

ANGELA: Do you know why I'm telling you about that theatre? It was supposed to be mine. She, Ribera, was going to give it to me. As a kind of inheritance. But I never got it. I don't know where it ended up. (*Pause. SHE pours herself another whisky.*)

GIRL: Just a bit for me, too, please.

ANGELA: A bit! What else do you want me to tell you? Something concrete? I'm sure you're all ears for specifics.

GIRL: I don't know what it could be. After all you've told me . . .

ANGELA: If you wish, I'll turn off the faucet.

GIRL: No! It's just that I wasn't expecting . . . exactly what you've been telling me . . .

ANGELA: And I haven't finished.

GIRL: Please, continue.

ANGELA: There were exactly four of us in that class who showed promise. We were going to conquer the world, and Empar Ribera had the key to that world. As it turned out, she wanted to direct a play before she retired completely from the scene. It was going to be her last great production. She had appeared in a lot of crap in her time, but, of course, this one had to be the real thing. She chose *Iphigenia in Aulis*. And she decided that one of the four of us would be Iphigenia. She was a real bitch.

GIRL: What did she do?

ANGELA: She pretended she couldn't decide which of us she wanted.

GIRL: She'd already made her choice from the start?

ANGELA: Of course! One of us had become her lover. Anna. Her name was Anna. Poor child. Ribera dazzled her, possessed her like a vampire, brainwashed her, and took her to bed.

GIRL: But if . . . they loved each other . . .

ANGELA: What are you talking about? A lovely girl of twenty, full of dreams, with her whole life before her, and that painted old scarecrow touching her, dirtying her . . . She was dying and she wouldn't accept it, she wouldn't give up. She wouldn't! Anna had to be Iphigenia. Well, it was a gift to the little whore! She played with the four of us, pretending that she hadn't decided . . . "Forgive me, I don't like to make you suffer. I know you're impatient for my decision . . ." Impatient, shit! One day I caught Anna alone. We were friends. The four of us were close. Like the four musketeers. We could speak without any ifs and buts. So I let her have it: "What kind of fucking game are you playing?" And she answered: "You can't understand, you can't. Empar . . . Empar . . ." Oh, sure, Empar . . . Empar Ribera. Great God in heaven! And then Anna grabbed my arm and assured me—in all her innocence!—that her relationship with the Egyptian mummy had nothing to do with the decision about who would play Iphigenia. And she actually believed it! I swear she did! I couldn't help laughing and she got very offended. I gave up on her, though something deep inside me was telling me not to, that I should insist, that I should free her from the claws that were holding on to her. And so, of course, she was convinced that she owed it exclusively to her talent as an actress. (*Pause.*) So? Will all that help you perform on stage the youthful illusions of the distinguished Empar Ribera?

GIRL: I don't know.

ANGELA: You can bet your pretty ass it will! I've told you all this, and I don't talk just to hear myself talk. Oh, well . . . (SHE *pours herself another shot of whisky.*) Forgive me if I got carried away.

GIRL: No, no . . .

ANGELA: I'll be sorry later. I suffer from insomnia. My bedmate snores and snores, sweetly at peace with the whole universe, and I, beside him, with my eyes wide open, I replay my whole day, I recognize my sins, and I set up a plan for improvement. My first sin is that I don't know when to keep my mouth shut. Not even with you, a stranger who'll start telling all the shocking things that funny Angela let slip while she was getting drunk on expensive whisky.

GIRL: I swear to you that no one will ever know!

ANGELA: Don't swear when you don't mean it. It's not worth it. It's not your fault I have a loose tongue. I resolve to keep my mouth shut, to pretend I'm mute, and within five minutes I'm shooting off my mouth again.

GIRL: I'm very grateful for your trust. I don't intend to abuse it, Miss Roca.

ANGELA: Would you please just call me Angela?

GIRL: Yes!

ANGELA: No. Not if it doesn't seem right to you. I'm not forcing you. I must seem much older to you, distant . . .

GIRL: You're not old, Miss Roca! (*Pause.*) I'm sorry . . . Angela.

ANGELA: An older woman who tells interesting stories, stories about things that happened a thousand years ago. Where were we? Now we have Anna preparing for the big event. The other three of us were trying not to be envious. We were young and nice girls. I needed to work so I started sending out resumes to see if any company would give me a job. I knew that, come what may, I wouldn't be playing Iphigenia. That dream came true for others, for me it was face reality. One day, la Ribera, who still loved us very much, invited us to a rehearsal. That's known as mental cruelty. And we went, naturally. In silence, intimidated, we sat in a corner while actors and actresses we'd criticized and admired were responding to la Ribera's baton. And Anna in the middle of it all. She saw us and greeted us from a distance. Afterwards, in deep concentration, she began to speak her lines and to move about the space that represented the stage. At first she was cold. Ribera had directed her to be. Then she got into the part. She grew more intense. I experienced a sudden attack of envy that I tried to keep from showing. I couldn't believe my eyes. She got better and better, and for an instant she really was Iphigenia. They've taught you at drama school that theatre is the essence of all the arts, right? Well, Anna was sculpture, painting, music, dance . . . and all this because she was Iphigenia! (*Pause.*) Oh, now I'm sounding like Gloria Marc. (*Pause.*) We were witnessing the birth of an actress. But Ribera still wasn't getting all she wanted from her. They told us that she never stopped demanding. A few days later, during another rehearsal—this time we weren't there, of course—Anna suddenly fell to the floor like a limp rag. She had fainted. Fright, a lot of commotion, did she need a doctor or didn't she . . . When she came to, Ribera asked the rest of the company to leave them alone. She and Anna, alone. The last person to leave heard Ribera ask in a dry tone: "What's the meaning of this faint?" And Anna replied: "I can't; I'll never be able to." They were alone together for more than an hour. Afterwards, Anna left without speaking to anyone. Everybody knows the rest. Anna was scared. She had taken on a responsibility she couldn't live up to. She said she was leaving the play, giving up the role. Then, instead of helping her, Ribera destroyed her. She told her that she was nobody and that she'd never amount to anything in the theatre. That she was finished before she'd ever begun. (*Pause.*) Anna, in that situation, didn't turn to anyone who could help her. Not even to us. Maybe she was ashamed and didn't dare. Perhaps. And the next day—or two days later, I'm not sure—she had the accident.

GIRL: An accident? She didn't get sick?

ANGELA: An accident. That is, she committed suicide.

GIRL: No!

ANGELA: Of course she did! Then . . . I'm not sure exactly what happened then. My memory's not so good for small details. They stopped the rehearsals. Empar Ribera began to negotiate with my friend Gloria Marc. Gloria was a match for Ribera; indeed she was. Cold and hard as a rock. She took Anna's place. And she was quite good. She established herself as a dramatic actress and I played maids for years. They say that theatre is a parable of life, but actually there's nothing in life that isn't a parable of life.

GIRL: You've . . . left me speechless. I don't know what to say.

ANGELA: I played maids, took part in strikes, believed that theatre had the power to educate. And a lot of other silly shit. Look, I can't complain. I've done all right. After all the walk-ons, I started getting better roles. But we aren't here to talk about me. You want me to tell you about Empar Ribera. I don't know what else to say. She was a good actress. They wouldn't like her today. But in the style of her time she was very good. Anything else?

GIRL: No. I've already taken too much of your time.

ANGELA: Ever since you got here you've said nothing but polite clichés. Do I frighten you so much?

GIRL: Of course not. I guess I'm a bit timid . . .

ANGELA: We actors are all timid. Do you have to read again for the part before you'll know if you have it?

GIRL: I won't get the part!

ANGELA: Of course you will! Those lousy auditions don't mean anything.

GIRL: For the first one I had to read a scene cold, without ever having seen the script. So who knows how I did. For the second one I have to recite from memory a scene from a play I've chosen myself.

ANGELA: And what play have you chosen?

Pause.

GIRL: *Iphigenia in Aulis.*

Pause.

ANGELA: (*Slowly.*) What a coincidence . . . You're just a bundle of surprises.

GIRL: I know you don't care for tragedies.

ANGELA: And why did you choose that one?

GIRL: I like it. The girl who is willing to be sacrificed for the good of her people . . .

ANGELA: (*With a leap.*) What??

GIRL: Iphigenia.

ANGELA: Iphigenia isn't willing to be sacrificed for anybody's good. Where did you get that silly idea?

GIRL: From the play.

ANGELA: Oh, do forgive me. I can see that you're an expert. That explains the scene from *Iphigenia*. Fancy that. I can't get very enthusiastic about Greek tragedy, but I do know this one by heart. Iphigenia is a poor fool and her father's a military son of a bitch who wants to fuck his neighbor's wife and take his land! A son of a bitch who'll step right over his daughter's body if he has to! And, naturally, she wants to live. But we hear nothing about that. They fill her head with all this crap and what can she do? She ends up going to her sacrifice like a lamb to slaughter. But just before the knife slices into her neck, she lets out this desperate cry from the depths of her soul: "Goodbye, light that I loved!" Where did I put the play? (SHE *starts looking among the books.*) It's here somewhere. Here it is! (SHE *takes a very worn book from the shelf.*) Iphigenia says, very clearly, exactly what she thinks just before they do her in. Look, here, read it!

GIRL: There's no need . . . really.

ANGELA: Read it! So that I can hear you!

The GIRL *stands up nervously, with book in hand, trying to read with feeling, with controlled passion.*

GIRL: "If, my father, I could find the words . . ."

ANGELA: She's talking to her bastard of a father to move him, to keep him from killing her.

GIRL: ". . . if I had the art of eloquence, I'd use it now. But the only art I have is my tears, and so with tears I must implore you."

ANGELA: The poor thing doesn't seem too happy.

GIRL: "Don't make me die so soon. The glow of life is sweet and I fear the darkness of death."

ANGELA: So tell me if she's so gung ho to sacrifice herself for the supposed good of her people!

GIRL: "I was your first child. I was the first to sit on your knees and receive your caresses. And you would say: One day I'll see you happy with your husband, and you'll bear grandchildren worthy of me. And I'd reply: When you're old, I'll take you gently into my palace and repay you for your efforts and the anguish you endured while raising me. How well I remember all that we said! But now you have forgotten and you want to kill me!"

ANGELA: "Now you have forgotten and you want to kill me ...!" Stronger ...! (SHE *grabs the book.*)You're the right age and have the voice for it, but I have the energy. (SHE *half reads, half recites from memory, with rage.*) "By the mother who bore me, what have I to do with your war? Oh, father, if I can't convince you, kiss me at least as I die and let me keep this memory of you!" And now she turns to her young brother, who's also there and watching. "Brother, there's little you can do to help me, but with your tears implore our father to let your sister live! Look at him, father, how he begs silently! Respect me, you bastard" —I've added "you bastard" to the script— "Respect me and have pity on my youth! Look at the light, father. For humankind it is the sweetest thing that exists; under the earth there is nothing at all. Only a madman wants to die: better a bad life a thousand times than a beautiful death!" (*Pause.* SHE *closes the book.*) That's Iphigenia. So forget about all the other crap! (SHE *puts the book away.*) Who's been giving you bad advice? (*The* GIRL *is silent.*) Do it my way and the role is yours. Whisky?

GIRL: Yes.

LIGHTS DOWN

SCENE FIVE

Lights up. Elements of a bland interior. Books. A telephone. In the background the bare walls of the stage. MARIA *receives the* GIRL, *who enters empty-handed.*

MARIA: Come in. Come in and sit down.

GIRL: I meant to bring you some flowers . . .

MARIA: You shouldn't even think of it. At least you didn't.

GIRL: I've had a hectic day. When I finally had a chance, the shops were all closed.

MARIA: Flowers are for divas. I wouldn't know what to do with them. Sit down. What would you like to drink?

GIRL: Nothing, for now. You asked me to call you Maria, didn't you?

MARIA: I hope you will. When are your auditions for the role of Empar Ribera?

GIRL: I had the last one yesterday.

MARIA: Oh? And how did it go?

GIRL: They're going to call me and let me know if I get the part.

MARIA: I haven't been much help. It's all the same. I wouldn't have been able to contribute much.

GIRL: You still can. In case they choose me, of course. And even if they don't , . . . I need someone who . . . I need someone to advise me . . .

MARIA: Of course. If I can, I will.

GIRL: And I've given them your telephone number. Do you mind?

MARIA: Not at all.

GIRL: I gave it to the director's assistant. If I'm to be the one, and he doesn't get me at home, he'll call me here.

MARIA: Well, we'll be listening for the phone to ring. A bit of a bother, isn't it?

GIRL: Yes. But what could I do?

MARIA: I'm expecting a call, too. But mine's from my doctor.

GIRL: Health problems?

MARIA: They have to give me the results of some tests I had. Well, we'll try to talk, relax, and forget about the phone. Do you know what I think? A drink would help. Even if we don't really want it. Then come what may.

GIRL: It sounds like a good idea.

MARIA: Can I fix you a whisky?

GIRL: Double. And three cubes, if you don't mind.

MARIA: Three for you and three for me. (*Pause.*) So, shall we talk about Empar Ribera or just tell her to get lost.

GIRL: I prefer to talk about her.

MARIA: Very well. You start. Ask me a question.

GIRL: There was a little theatre, a toy theatre, red, blue, and gold . . .

MARIA: How did you know that?

GIRL: I have one like it. Don't you remember? I told you about it when we first talked.

MARIA: Empar Ribera's toy theatre?

GIRL: Mine. And another one that you had. Empar Ribera's . . . I think she said that she would give it to Angela Roca. As a kind of inheritance. But then she didn't . . .

MARIA: Are you saying that Empar Ribera told Angela Roca that she would give her the toy theatre? Where did you get that idea? (*Silence.*) Angela! You've been talking with Angela, haven't you?

GIRL: Yes.

MARIA: As a kind of inheritance . . . ! She never collected that inheritance! What else did Angela tell you?

GIRL: Does it bother you that I talked with her?

MARIA: On the contrary!

GIRL: I wanted to know what Empar Ribera was like, and I got the idea that certain people could tell me. You, Angela, and . . . well, Gloria Marc, too.

MARIA: Ah! So that one granted you an audience.

GIRL: Yes.

MARIA: Fantastic! And what can I possibly add to what they must have told you?

GIRL: Their memories of her seem different. To contradict each other.

MARIA: Really? Let's see, tell me which of their memories are contradictory.

GIRL: They ended up confusing me. It's not that they really contradict each other. Well, at first glance, yes, but . . . they both agree that Ribera was a great actress. Both of them spoke to me fondly of the evenings they spent at her house as members of a special group of four, the best in the class. For Gloria Marc that was . . . one of the most important experiences of her life. She called it a golden age. For Angela Roca it was a kind of disappointment, but you could tell that it had been a great time for her, too.

MARIA: It was a great time for all of us.

GIRL: Only . . . maybe love of the theatre wasn't the only reason Empar Ribera invited you to her house. Is that true?

MARIA: I don't know. Go on.

GIRL: Apparently, the other girl, Anna, became her lover. Then she gave her the role of Iphigenia but demanded as lot from her, as she'd always demanded of herself. Angela says that maybe the girl would have been a good Iphigenia if Ribera hadn't paralyzed her with so many demands. Finally, she committed suicide. Right?

MARIA: Oh boy! What a piece of soap opera.

GIRL: It wasn't that way?

MARIA: First, finish your story.

GIRL: And then Gloria Marc substituted for your dead friend.

MARIA: Yes.

GIRL: And that was the beginning of her career.

MARIA: But indeed. And how was it that Ribera chose Gloria to take Anna's place?

GIRL: Because she thought that she was the best, or . . . because Gloria was the only one of you who was bold enough to offer herself.

MARIA: Have you finished? Now will you let me give you my version of the events?

GIRL: I'm dying to hear.

MARIA: It may be true that Ribera demanded more of Anna than the poor girl could give. She loved her. But don't jump to conclusions, she loved all four of us. Maybe Anna a little more than the others; maybe she saw in her the successor she was looking for. In her more than in the rest of us. But I doubt that there was ever any kind of sex between them. It's all the same to me, but I don't think so. The truth is I never understood Empar Ribera very well. She spent those two years reliving her own youth through us. She didn't have much time left, I suppose she was aware of that, and she clung to four girls in whom she saw talent as actresses. She was a very hard woman but she also had her sentimental side. The toy theatre proves that.

GIRL: Why the toy theatre?

MARIA: It was, perhaps, her most beloved possession. Her brother had given it to her. On the curtain were the two initials E and R.

GIRL: Do you know what became of it?

MARIA: Better than anyone. In some way that theatre symbolized, with its sets, with its little figures, with the affection of the person who had given it to her . . . with all that, the toy theatre symbolized for her THE THEATRE, in capital letters, or unwritten in any letters large or small. And she decided to give it to the one she considered her heir. She had said so many times. And she said it once more the day she announced that she wanted to direct *Iphigenia* and then retire for good. I've already said that besides being hard and very demanding, she was above all a sentimental person . . . and since she also had a touch of bad taste, or was simply old-fashioned, she delighted in theatrical gestures. So, with a very solemn face, she announced: "I cannot divide the theatre into four parts. I'll send it and the one who receives it will know that she is my Iphigenia."

GIRL: But she'd already decided that Anna would get the role!

MARIA: What do you know about it?

GIRL: Angela Roca was convinced.

MARIA: Angela likes to think it was that way. But until Anna actually received an enormous box with the theatre inside, the four of us spent several days on pins and needles, hugging one another and swearing that we'd always be friends no matter who won. Anna won and I just about died of envy. I've never envied anyone so much. (*Pause.*) And that envy has never left me.

Pause. MARIA *makes a strange gesture.*

GIRL: Are you all right?

MARIA: I got carried away a little. And it's not good for me. (*Pause.*)

The rehearsals began for *Iphigenia in Aulis*. We went to one. Anna hadn't quite gotten into the part.

GIRL: Wasn't she magnificent in that rehearsal?

MARIA: No. It was early on. They were still trying different things. But Anna was impatient with herself. She wanted to be completely into the character. She was suffering. I don't know how she would have been eventually. Perhaps very good, who knows. And then the accident happened.

GIRL: The suicide.

MARIA: Forget about suicide. It was an accident. She was riding in a car with some other members of the company. She was in the back seat. Her door wasn't closed properly. When they went around a curve, she leaned too hard on the door and it flew open . . . and she fell out. Her head hit the pavement and she died instantly.

GIRL: And what if she did throw herself out?

MARIA: Why? (*Pause.*) No, life isn't a melodrama. (*Pause.*)Gloria, Angela, and I, when we found out, called one another and made plans to get together, and . . . that was a time of despair for us. Our world was falling apart. If life was over for our friend, it was ending for us, too. I don't remember where we were. I don't know in whose house. We cried and hugged, we were united, and suddenly we felt grown up. The monster, as Angela would say, had left a mark that would make us different from other mortals. There was a morbid complacency in our grief. Then a door opened and in came Empar Ribera. She was carrying a large package. At first she said nothing; she just stood there looking at us. We couldn't say anything either. Have you ever seen a face that's totally drained of emotion? Ribera's face was drained of feeling. Not a tear. We never saw her cry. But Anna's death had hit her hard. Very hard. Finally, she said she felt tired, sat down, and placed the package beside her. She began to speak in a low voice. She didn't mention Anna directly. She didn't need to prove anything. I remember that I was looking at her and feeling ashamed that my grief wasn't the same. I looked at her and thought: it's finished for Empar Ribera. It's all over. That's why I was surprised when I caught the sense of the words that the old actress was saying with no expression whatsoever; she was saying that the rehearsal for *Iphigenia* couldn't be delayed, that there were only two weeks left until opening night. That, obviously, one of us had to take over the role. That she didn't have the will to make another choice and that we should decide among ourselves who it would be. She got up with some effort and pointed to the package: "That's the toy theatre," she uttered. "I retrieved it from Anna's house. Now . . . tell me who gets it and I'll know who has to begin to rehearse this afternoon." Then she dragged herself to the door.

GIRL: Gloria and Angela didn't tell me this part of the story. Neither of them did.

MARIA: Memory lapses, I guess! It's a problem we all have sometimes, so you'll have to forgive them. When we were alone, I was the first to react. Let them cancel the production; what was that old witch thinking of! A minute before, I was dying of shame because my feelings at Anna's death were nothing compared to hers, and now I didn't understand what was happening. And my indignation was growing by leaps and bounds. I don't know what other things I said, but I didn't stop talking for quite a while. Finally, I did shut up. My friends had nothing to say either. In fact, they hadn't even opened their mouths. Then, one of them, I don't remember which, began saying that the play would open whether we liked it or not. There was no way we could prevent it. And taking on Anna's role would be the best tribute we could pay her. After a moment they were both talking at the same time, stepping on each other's words and one of them finishing the sentences the other had begun. It seemed that they were reading each other's thoughts and that they were in perfect agreement. It all came down to this: since as a matter of honor none of us wanted to give up our chance, the only solution was to gamble to see who'd get the toy theatre.

GIRL: What do you mean?

MARIA: Leave it to chance. Draw straws, toss a coin, or play a game of cards.

GIRL: Wasn't there any other way?

MARIA: Only if two of us bowed out gracefully.

GIRL: (*Understanding.*) Ah, I guess there wasn't an easy way out.

MARIA: (*Dryly.*) But I didn't participate!

GIRL: (*Taken by surprise.*) Really?

MARIA: I refused to take part in the card game they'd decided on. But that didn't stop them. (SHE *looks into the* GIRL's *eyes and smiles.*) You would have taken your chance too.

GIRL: I don't know.

MARIA: And we'll never know. They played their game for the toy theatre, and the role that went with it, with real enthusiasm, eyes gleaming, each wanting the other to disappear . . . the two great friends would have killed for that role. Gloria won and Angela lost. They didn't tell you that part of the story, but they remember it. They remember it so well that they've never worked together again. And they never will. (*Pause. Change of tone.*) Empar Ribera used to say that theatre had to be one man or one woman, the actor, who consoles another man or woman, the spectator. Actors are there to console the audience. Empar Ribera, who was neither angel or devil, wanted to convince us that we were going to be a kind of priestess, a kind of holy person celebrating beneficial rites on the stage. I didn't see myself capable of any of that; but, at times, I think that Anna, who was so close to her mentor, came to really believe it. Gloria and Angela certainly didn't. They wanted the theatre to show off their narcissism shamelessly on stage. In the theatre, the heroines cry, they despair, their lovers abandon them . . . but they aren't alone. They still have the audience . . . Whatever happens Gloria and Angela will always have the audience and hear the applause.

GIRL: Are you judging them or actors in general?

MARIA: I'm talking about my two friends. And you know, they're good at what they do. They're very good actresses. And do you want to know something else? It doesn't matter what they think or want. The real truth is they always achieve what Empar Ribera attempted: their performances console the spectator.

Pause.

GIRL: And you?

MARIA: Me? What about me? I wasn't a real actress. If I had been I would have tried to get that toy theatre. I hate them. And I love them. I admire them. And most of all . . . I've already told you this: I know that they envy each other, but I envy them both infinitely more. Maybe, without realizing it, I'm lying too when I talk about them. You don't have to take my word. I envied them that day when they were playing cards for the role of Iphigenia. I envied them so much that I stole the toy theatre.

GIRL: You?

MARIA: Yes. Afterwards, I stole it. The little theatre disappeared and Gloria didn't get it. I don't know if it ever mattered to her.

GIRL: But you don't have it!

MARIA: How do you know? No, I don't have it.

GIRL: What did you do with it?

MARIA: It was burning my fingers. It wasn't mine. It didn't belong to me. But I didn't want to return it. I couldn't. For a few years I worked as an actress. I got parts and I managed. But one thing was missing. I wasn't bitch enough to really be first rate. I got into film dubbing . . . It took me farther and farther away from the stage . . . Then, one day, I took the toy theatre and sold it for half what it was worth.

Pause.

GIRL: And it was then that my parents bought it and gave it to me as a gift.

MARIA: Gave it to you?

GIRL: If it's not the one I have, at least it's just like the one you and Angela have described.

MARIA: A red curtain with two initials?

GIRL: E. R.

MARIA: (*Laughs.*) That really is funny! You can be sure that the role of Empar Ribera will be yours. It's predestined!

GIRL: Don't make fun of me.

MARIA: Don't you believe it, too?

GIRL: Yes. (*Change of tone.*) Ever since I came here, and now especially, I've wanted to ask you what I should do with the toy theatre. Should I take it to Gloria Marc? First I thought of Angela Roca, but maybe it's more appropriate to return it to Gloria. She was the one who won it.

MARIA: It's yours. Keep it.

GIRL: You're sure?

MARIA: Absolutely. Keep it, remember it's history, and go on to become a great, great actress.

Pause.

GIRL: All right, I will. I'll be a great actress and I'll also do *Iphigenia in Aulis*.

MARIA: Of course!

GIRL: (*Growing enthusiastic.*) I'll be that girl who wants to live, who wants light, but who ends up accepting sacrifice, who ends up accepting her role: innocence sacrificed.

MARIA: (*Realistic.*) Cut the sacrifice! In the last minute of the play, a god arrives, or someone, and carries her off through the air. And she ends up in Tauris, a seaport, where she becomes a bloodthirsty priestess who kills all the foreigners who stray too close to the coast.

GIRL: That's another tragedy.

MARIA: Part Two of the same one, written by the same author. This one is Iphigenia, too. If you do play the part someday, don't make her innocent. Do it well and that will be sufficient.

GIRL: (*Disconcerted.*) But who is Iphigenia really?

MARIA: When the day comes, it will be you.

The telephone rings. Signs of anxiety in both women. MARIA goes and picks up.

MARIA: Hello . . .

GIRL: For me?

MARIA: (*Shakes her head.*) You have the results of my tests? (*To the phone.*) Positive, right . . . ? Thank you . . . Yes. I will, tomorrow.

GIRL: Good news?

MARIA: The cancer has spread. They won't be able to operate.

LIGHTS DOWN

SCENE SIX

The stage is now completely bare. All traces of the set have disappeared. ANGELA, in street attire, waits leaning against a wall, calmly and in silence. The sound of footsteps. GLORIA, also in street wear, enters and crosses the stage briskly without noticing ANGELA.

GLORIA: (*In a loud voice toward the side of the stage where SHE has just entered.*) See you tomorrow! I love you all! Goodnight everyone!

ANGELA steps forward so that GLORIA can see her.

ANGELA: How do you do it?

GLORIA *stops at a prudent distance.* THEY *look at each other.*

ANGELA: Isn't it exhausting to always say what's convenient and never what you really feel? When will you stop embellishing your own character? Still, it must be a good system. It's certainly worked great for you.

Pause.

GLORIA: Did you go to the funeral?

ANGELA: That's where I've come from.

GLORIA *takes a deep breath.*

GLORIA: Did the flowers I sent arrive?

ANGELA: They were in the best of taste.

GLORIA: This damn matinee kept me from going. (*Pause.*) There no way I could get out of it.

ANGELA: She wanted to give us a lesson. She loved to spend her life giving lessons. (*Lowering her voice.*) And to the monster, too.

GLORIA: What are you doing here?

ANGELA: I came to annoy you.

GLORIA: What an honor!

ANGELA: When will you be through with this?

GLORIA: Through with what?

ANGELA: This one-woman show. How much longer does it go on?

GLORIA: Two weeks more and it closes.

ANGELA: And after that, are you going on tour?

GLORIA: Yes. But a short one. We'll see. I'm feeling lazy.

ANGELA: She was admitted to the hospital a week ago. She wouldn't let them tell anyone. She refused phone calls, too.

GLORIA: Years ago I learned that if I didn't look out for myself no one else would. And I've managed quite well. At least I didn't go around sermonizing. I'm not a hypocrite.

ANGELA: How about frigid? You aren't frigid?

GLORIA: Not all the men who've passed through my life have given me the same pleasure. Some didn't give me any at all.

ANGELA: I knew that no one, ever, would do anything for me, but I didn't want to think that I was working just for my career and nothing else. There had to be something bigger, that would include other things and other people.

GLORIA: Don't make me laugh. You've walked over all the bodies when it suited you.

ANGELA: If I ever walked over anybody, it was in self-defense. Just like you.

Long Pause.

GLORIA: I remember so many things. Our first trip to Paris. That first year at drama school, Anna, Maria, you, me, your brother . . . Something else. I once stole a book from the Joy of Reading Bookstore, and now nobody even knows that the Joy of Reading Bookstore ever existed.

ANGELA: Which would be better? To die first or to live while the others die off?

GLORIA: Living is always the best, stupid.

ANGELA: You're the only left who can remind me of that trip to Paris. If you die before I do, something I dearly hope, no one will ever speak to me about it again. More and more empty spaces. Until a moment ago we still had Maria . . .

GLORIA: She started out with promise, but soon you could see that she wasn't a good actress.

ANGELA: Mediocre at best. But she didn't seem so bad at first.

GLORIA: She wasn't an actress. Period. She lacked sensitivity.

ANGELA: No, it wasn't that.

GLORIA: Not as a person but for performing. That's what I think. Maybe she was adequate as a director. I suppose we'll never know.

ANGELA: What are we going to do without her?

Pause.

GLORIA: We're both better equipped for the stage.

ANGELA: At least we got further. You with your screaming and me trying to give a true picture of life.

GLORIA: It must be very difficult to become respected throughout Europe simply by screaming.

ANGELA: I was satisfied with my career. If I were born again, I'd do it all the same. Until today. When I was playing maids, I thought: "It doesn't matter; someday I'll show them what I'm capable of, and all these people around me will fall on their asses and be sorry they didn't notice me . . ." I wasn't counting on the monster. I've shown them that I'm somebody, perhaps, but all those I wanted to prove it to have disappeared. They're not here. They're my ghosts. I can't expect a ghost to fall on its ass. A girl came to ask me things about Empar Ribera . . .

GLORIA: She came to see me, too.

ANGELA: I talked a lot. Too much. Then I realized that she didn't get what I was saying. Really, that girl didn't understand me. She didn't have the points of reference. I don't know how Ribera managed to connect the way she did with us.

GLORIA: She knew that I was a loner. That was fundamental with me. If you had chosen, like me, to be alone from the start, it wouldn't seem so strange to you now. (*Pause.*) I suppose everyone's alone. And each of us manages as best we can. I have the theatre.

ANGELA: And what about me? What do I have? Shit?

GLORIA: What do you feel when the lights come up and you have to go out on the stage?

ANGELA: What do I feel? Terror. I shouldn't have come on stage.

GLORIA: Even today?

ANGELA: The last time I acted in a theatre, more than ever.

GLORIA: It's the same with me. And it's wonderful. Your own fear, your terror, right there beside you on this side of the lights. And on the other side the skeptical or hopeful expectations of the bastards who've paid to see you. I've never lost that sensation from the very first day. I walk out into the light and vomit up my terror at them, I vomit a story that takes form as my fear is turned into words.

ANGELA: If I'm lucky, and I often am, those gazes from the other side help me to get through to the end. No, they're not bastards.

GLORIA: But you're defenseless up there before them. And they can really screw you. I go out, I regurgitate my lines, they are certain to applaud me, but I'm still alone. But, why not? I've gained something. It's enough just to keep going. You said that yourself.

ANGELA: To keep going during the performance. Not afterwards. But you do. You have the energy and you can exchange Sean for another lover. If not, you wouldn't be Gloria Marc. I've lost. It's over. I don't know if I can ever do theatre again.

GLORIA: What? What are you saying?

ANGELA: You heard me.

GLORIA: You're joking, aren't you?

ANGELA: No, I don't believe I'll act on the stage again. It's finished. I don't intend to return to the theatre! And it's of no concern to you!

GLORIA: Then, why have you come? To tell me you're not going to return to the theatre, even when it's of no concern to me? I suppose if you've come here it must be for something!

ANGELA: I came to tell you that I'm vanishing, that I'm going away, like the others. That you're staying behind. The whole stage for your own little self. And when you finish and start to leave don't forget to turn off the lights. There's no one left behind you.

Pause.

GLORIA: Oh, no! You can't do that to me!

ANGELA: There's nothing more to say. So . . . enjoy yourself!

GLORIA: You can't do this to me! Wait!

ANGELA: Send me a postcard!

GLORIA: Wait, you bitch, wait! You're not alone!

ANGELA *stops.*

ANGELA: What?

GLORIA: (*Nervously.*) You aren't alone.

ANGELA: Oh, no? What mathematical formula did you use to decide that?

GLORIA: You're not alone because I'm still here.

ANGELA: You? So what?

GLORIA: I need you, the same as you need me. I need to know that you're here; I want to be able to think every time I get a good review that you're reading it and getting terribly pissed off; I want to have the feeling that I'm beating you in the game; I also want you to be able to hurt me from time to time. I want to be able to feel hurt from something you've said, to be irritated by what you're thinking and what you're doing. You're the only one who can still judge me. And I'm the only one who can judge you. If we no longer have that . . . But we still do. (*Louder.*) What more do you want me to say? Damn you! You know it perfectly well! You know it and damn you to hell!

ANGELA: My! Your tragic side has come out! What can the lady who's so devoted to being alone be up to now?

GLORIA: I don't want you to leave the theatre, I won't permit it, and you don't want to either. You're scared, that's all. You don't dare ask me what you want to ask me and so you're trying blackmail. All right, you won't leave the theatre because you'll be on stage with me.

ANGELA: I, with you?

GLORIA: How many times do I have to repeat it? You didn't come to tell me you're leaving the theatre! You came to tell me that you'll work with me!

ANGELA: God, what a revelation! I can't believe my ears! Really? Maybe I'll think about it. Would we actually work together?

GLORIA: For a while. Until the wounds heal. We'll do the Ibsen play that Maria was going to direct.. You like Ibsen, don't you?

ANGELA: He's halfway between you and me.

Pause.

GLORIA: Then?

ANGELA: We'll have to find another director.

GLORIA: That's no problem. They're always looking for work. They'll be waiting in line for us.

ANGELA: We won't get along. We'll fight. Just seeing you can unhinge me. It has to be clear in the contract that, wherever we play, we have to have separate dressing rooms. (*Pause.*) Yes, we'll do the play. (*Pause.*) Thank you.

GLORIA: Oh, go to hell!

ANGELA: Thanks, bitch, thanks.

GLORIA: (*Changing suddenly to a lighter tone.*) We could even do a benefit performance from time to time, couldn't we?

ANGELA: A benefit, eh? Wait until the reviews come out.

GLORIA: Oh, the critics are certain to favor you. They love to surprise people.

ANGELA: You'll survive it . . . But we have to have a good Borkman. Otherwise, it's off.

GLORIA: After our last dinner together, Maria was convinced we'd never work on stage together.

ANGELA: In a way she was right. She'll never see us work together.

The GIRL enters with a certain timidity. SHE has a large box in her hands, and only her head shows over it. SHE stops. SHE looks at them. ANGELA and GLORIA are suddenly silent and THEY look at her, too, coldly, without inviting her to step forward.

GIRL: I'm sorry. I've interrupted your conversation.

Pause.

ANGELA: Yes, but it doesn't matter.

GIRL: I didn't know I'd find you together.

GLORIA: Were you coming to see me?

GIRL: Yes . . . maybe it's better that you're both here . . . It's a very sad moment, isn't it? . . . I knew your friend Maria. I didn't expect her to die so soon.

ANGELA: You mean you didn't expect her to die at all.

GIRL: I spoke with her. She told me that she was going to die.

ANGELA: (*Brusquely.*) Told you?

GIRL: Yes.

GLORIA: (*Rapidly.*) Why have you come, dear?

GIRL: I have a gift for you.

GLORIA: (*Nicer.*) For me?

GIRL: I suppose so. I suppose it has to be for you. Although Miss Roca also has some right to it.

SHE *looks all around and ends up leaving the box on the floor.* SHE *begins to open it.*

GLORIA: What is it?

GIRL: One moment.

SHE *takes from the box an old, faded toy theatre of beautiful workmanship.* SHE *holds it up.*

GLORIA: A toy theatre?

ANGELA: Be quiet. It's very similar . . . don't you see? It looks like Empar Ribera's.

GLORIA: It can't be.

GIRL: I think it is Ribera's.

GLORIA: Where did you get it?

GIRL: I've always had it, since I was a child.

GLORIA *and* ANGELA *have come close.*

ANGELA: (*Pointing.*) The initials.

GLORIA: Yes, it is hers.

ANGELA: My God!

THEY *raise the curtain—faded dark vermillion—and look inside.*

GLORIA: The last thing I expected to see in my life. What detail! But now it's yours. You shouldn't give it away.

GIRL: I've decided to. I've decided that I don't have a right to keep it.

ANGELA: (*Excited, to the* GIRL.) And the little figures, are they still in their box? Take them out.

GIRL: I don't have them. They got lost. All of them.

(*Pause.*)

ANGELA: What good's a theatre without characters?

GLORIA: It's not a theatre anymore. It's only an object. (*Nicely, to the* GIRL.) I can't accept it. No way could I. It's yours. It's a beautiful object. The memories it brings back Right, Angela? But if you gave it to me, I'd give it back to you. I'm always on the go, and it would only gather dust.

ANGELA: It has enough already.

GLORIA: It's better that you keep it. (*Offhandedly.*) Imagine that you've just inherited it.

GIRL: (*Disconcerted.*) I thought . . . (*To* ANGELA.) You don't want it either?

ANGELA: I? No, thank you. Much less without the little characters.

GIRL: But haven't you both wanted . . . very much . . . to have this theatre?

ANGELA: I don't remember . . . Yes.

GLORIA: You're talking about a long time ago . . . We can't take it from you.

ANGELA: (*Suddenly, to the* GIRL.) How are your rehearsals going?

GIRL: What rehearsals?

ANGELA: The rehearsals for the play about Empar Ribera, I suppose.

GIRL: Oh! The fact is . . . I didn't get the part.

GLORIA: No?

ANGELA: What a shame!

GLORIA: Oh, but I told you I'd talk to the director! I'm so absentminded! Don't worry. Lose one opportunity and another appears, you'll see.

GIRL: I don't know about that.

ANGELA: Well, I've got to be going.

GLORIA: I'll go out with you. (*To the* GIRL.) Many thanks, truly. It's your toy theatre. You have the right to it. Don't have any doubts about that. We'll see each other sometime. Now that I know you I'll be watching your career with interest. And someday . . . maybe we'll work together.

ANGELA: And do look for those little characters. Don't forget. Look for them.

THEY *make gestures of goodbye to the* GIRL *and start across the stage to exit.*

GLORIA: (*Glancing at the stage.*) We're on a stage and we're going to make our final exit. Who gets the last line? Or do we toss a coin for it?

ANGELA: No! I don't trust you! Anyhow, I don't want the last line, I want the best one.

GLORIA: Very well. In that case . . . we'll both exit . . . in silence. Scared to death, as always.

ANGELA: There's no reason to be afraid! As soon as we begin to speak we'll have them in our hands. We've done it so many times before. Do you remember my Juliet . . . ? "Wilt thou be gone? It is not yet near day. It was the nightingale and not the lark, that pierc'd the fearful hollow of thine ear. Nightly she sings on yond pomegranate tree. Believe me, love, it was the nightingale . . ."

GLORIA: Or what about my Nora . . . ? "Torvald, there would have to be a miracle and I don't believe in miracles. We would have to change too much for life between us to become a marriage. Goodbye!" Pumb!!

ANGELA: Goodbye? Then . . . "Goodbye, light that I've loved so much!"

GLORIA: No, you can't say that line. It doesn't belong just to you.

GLORIA AND ANGELA: (*Together.*) "Goodbye, light that I've loved so much!"

Their voices have faded away. Pause. The GIRL *remains still for a moment. Then* SHE *places the little theatre on the box.*

GIRL: No characters. They're lost. That's why I stopped playing with it.

Pause. SHE *strikes a match.* SHE *goes to the toy theatre and sets it on fire.* SHE *looks at it for a moment.* SHE *exits. The stage is almost dark. The toy theatre is burning. The play of flames creates light and moving shadows on the bare walls. Pause. Then, slowly, a beautiful purple curtain begins to descend, covering and hiding the stage and the toy theatre. In the lower right corner, the initials* E.R. *stand out in gold.*

LIGHTS DOWN

ACKNOWLEDGMENTS

A number of people have made a meaningful contribution to my efforts to bring Benet i Jornet's theatre to a wider English-speaking audience. I am grateful to directors Christopher Mack and Melanie Sutherland for their effective staged readings of *Stages* and *Fleeting*, to Daniel Gerould, Frank Hentschker, and Jan Stenzel of the Martin E. Segal Theatre Center for their oversight of the publication of the translations, and to Richard B. Medoff, who acted as a critical sounding board during the translation process. I am particularly indebted to Christopher Silsby, whose sensitivity, imagination, and editorial skills are reflected in so many ways in this book. I express my deepest gratitude to the Institut Ramon Llull for the translation grant that enabled the publication to go forward. And to the playwright himself, I say *moltes gràcies* for permission to translate his plays and for his unfailing patience and encouragement.

New York City
MPH
October, 2008

ABOUT THE TRANSLATOR

Marion Peter Holt is a writer, translator, and Professor Emeritus of Theatre and Spanish at the City University of New York. He also has been a visiting Professor of Theatre at the Yale School of Drama, Hunter College, and Barcelona's Institut del Teatre. Among his publications are: *The Contemporary Spanish Theatre (1949-1972)*, *Antonio Buero-Vallejo: Three Plays*, *DramaContemporary: Spain*, and *Magical Places, the Story of Spartanburg's Theatres and Their Entertainments: 1900-1950*. In 2002, his article "The Magical Montgomery" received the Jeffrey Weiss Award of the Theatre Historical Society of America. His translations of plays by Buero-Vallejo, López Rubio, Antonio Skármeta, Sergi Belbel, and other Spanish and Catalan playwrights have been performed in New York and London, in Australia, and by regional and university theatres in the United States and England, including Center Stage (Baltimore), The Wilma Theatre (Philadelphia), San Diego Repertory, Bailiwick Repertory (Chicago), and Atlanta's Alliance Theatre. He is member of the Dramatists Guild.

The Institut Ramon Llull has a mission to promote Catalan language and culture internationally, in all of its variations and methods of expression. In order to accomplish this task, it carries out the following activities:

a) Foster Catalan language classes in universities and other centers of higher learning, placing special emphasis on the study and research of Catalan language and culture beyond its linguistic domain.

b) Promote the teaching of Catalan to the general public beyond the linguistic domain.

c) Broaden the familiarization with Catalan literature on an international level by encouraging and supporting translations into other languages and corresponding promotional activities for such works when deemed appropriate.

d) Contribute to the international dissemination of works of philosophy, nonfiction, and research by providing encouragement and support for translations into other languages, organizing meetings, seminars and exchange programs, and other activities towards the advancement of the Catalan academic, intellectual, and scientific community abroad.

e) Promote and provide support to international Catalan societies in their initiatives, projects, and activities.

f) Further the international impact of Catalan visual arts through the use of appropriate promotional strategies and activities, encourage the internationalization of outstanding artistic work, provide aid towards the exposure of artists and artwork abroad, and broaden the international awareness of Catalonia's artistic patrimony.

g) Promote collaborations, projects, and joint initiatives with institutions and organizations dedicated to the diffusion of Catalan culture, whether within the boundaries of the linguistic domain or without; placing a special emphasis on the homologous institutions of other counties or cultures.

The Institut Ramon Llull carries out its activities in the areas of Language, Artistic Creation, and Humanities and Science.

Please check: http://www.llull.cat/_eng/_home/

The Martin E. Segal Theatre Center (MESTC), is a non-profit center for theatre, dance and film affiliated with CUNY's Ph.D. Program in Theatre. The Center's mission is to bridge the gap between academia and the professional performing arts communities both within the United States and internationally. By providing an open environment for the development of educational, community-driven, and professional projects in the performing arts, MESTC is a home to theatre scholars, students, playwrights, actors, dancers, directors, dramaturges, and performing arts managers from the local and international theatre communities. Through diverse programming—staged readings, theatre events, panel discussions, lectures, conferences, film screenings, dance—and a number of publications, MESTC enables artists, academics, visiting scholars and performing arts professionals to participate actively in the advancement and appreciation of the entire range of theatrical experience. The Center presents staged readings to further the development of new and classic plays, lecture series, televised seminars featuring professional and academic luminaries, and arts in education programs, and maintains its long-standing visiting scholars-from-abroad program. In addition, the Center publishes a series of highly-regarded academic journals, as well as books, including plays in translation, written, translated and edited by leading scholars. For more information, please visit http://web.gc.cuny.edu/mestc

The Graduate Center, CUNY, of which the Martin E. Segal Theatre Center is an integral part, is the doctorate-granting institution of The City University of New York (CUNY). An internationally recognized center for advanced studies and a national model for public doctoral education, the school offers more than thirty doctoral programs, as well as a number of master's programs. Many of its faculty members are among the world's leading scholars in their respective fields, and its alumni hold major positions in industry and government, as well as in academia. The Graduate Center is also home to twenty-eight interdisciplinary research centers and institutes focused on areas of compelling social, civic, cultural, and scientific concerns. Located in a landmark Fifth Avenue building, The Graduate Center has become a vital part of New York City's intellectual and cultural life with its extensive array of public lectures, exhibitions, concerts, and theatrical events.
To find out more, please visit: http://www.gc.cuny.edu

Ph.D. Program in Theatre, The Graduate Center, CUNY, is one of the leading doctoral theatre programs in the United States. Faculty includes distinguished professors, holders of endowed chairs, and internationally recognized scholars. The program trains future scholars and teachers in all the disciplines of theatre research. Faculty members edit MESTC publications, working closely with the doctoral students in theatre who perform a variety of editorial functions and learn the skills involved in the creation of books and journals.
For more information on the program, please visit: http://web.gc.cuny.edu/theatre

The MESTC Publication Wing produces both journals and individual volumes. Journals include *Slavic and Eastern European Performance* (SEEP), *The Journal of American Drama and Theatre* (JADT), and *Western European Stages* (WES). Books include *Four Melodramas by Pixérécourt* (edited by Daniel Gerould and Marvin Carlson—both Distinguished Professors of Theatre at the CUNY Graduate Center), *Contemporary Theatre in Egypt* (which includes the translation of three plays by Alfred Farag, Gamal Maqsoud, and Lenin El-Ramley, edited by Marvin Carlson), *The Heirs of Molière* (edited and translated by Marvin Carlson), *Seven Plays by Stanisław Ignacy Witkiewicz* (edited and translated by Daniel Gerould), *The Arab Oedipus: Four Plays* (edited by Marvin Carlson), *Theatre Research Resources in New York City* (edited by Jessica Brater, Senior Editor Marvin Carlson), and *Comedy: A Bibliography of Critical Studies in English on the Theory and Practice of Comedy in Drama, Theatre and Performance* (edited by Meghan Duffy, Senior Editor Daniel Gerould). New publications include: *BAiT-Buenos Aires in Translation: Four Plays* (edited and translated by Jean Graham-Jones), *roMANIA AFTER 2000: Five New Romanian Plays* (edited by Saviana Stanescu and Daniel Gerould), *Four Plays from North Africa* (edited by Marvin Carlson), and *Barcelona Plays: A Collection of New Plays by Catalan Playwrights* (edited and translated by Marion Peter Holt and Sharon G. Feldman).
To find out more, please visit: http://web.gc.cuny.edu/mestc/subscribe.htm